THE BASICS OF
ELECTRONICS

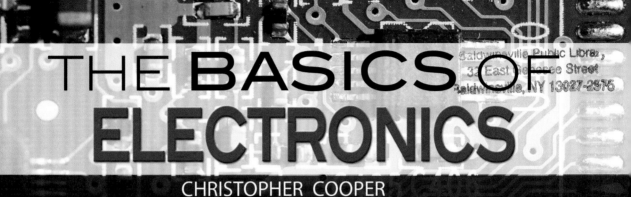

CORE CONCEPTS

THE BASICS OF ELECTRONICS

CHRISTOPHER COOPER

ROSEN
PUBLISHING®

New York

This edition published in 2015 by:

The Rosen Publishing Group, Inc.
29 East 21st Street
New York, NY 10010

Additional end matter copyright © 2015 by The Rosen Publishing Group, Inc.

MAY 2 2 2015

Library of Congress Cataloging-in-Publication Data

Cooper, Christopher.
The basics of electronics/by Christopher Cooper, first edition.
    p. cm.—(Core concepts)
Includes bibliographical references and index.
ISBN 978-1-4777-7756-5 (library binding)
1. Electronics—Juvenile literature. I. Cooper, Christopher
(Christopher E.) II. Title.
TK7820.C66 2015
621.381—d23

Manufactured in the United States of America

© 2004 Brown Bear Books Ltd.

CONTENTS

CHAPTER ONE

THE MIGHTY ELECTRON

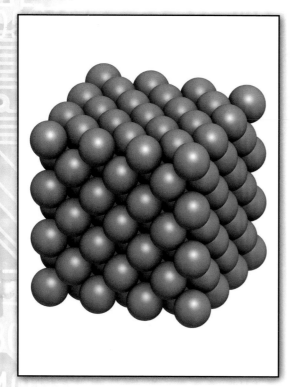

Shown here are the orderly ranks of atoms in a sample of gold. Each is about a hundred-millionth of the thickness of a fingernail.

The whole of modern electronics is built on the properties of one tiny particle that is found in the atoms of all elements—the electron. Little more than a century ago the electron was unknown. Now it has come to dominate modern technology.

At the end of the 19th century most physicists were convinced that chemical elements existed in the form of atoms—tiny units of matter that are normally undivided and indivisible. But nothing at all was known about their internal structure.

The first glimpse into the atom came when the English physicist William Crookes constructed a device called the Crookes tube. It was a glass bottle in which the air pressure could be reduced to a ten-thousandth of its normal value. Two electrodes protruded into the low-pressure gas. When a high voltage was applied across the electrodes, glowing colored patches and bands of light appeared in the tube. The light changed in complex ways as the pressure and voltage were altered.

FRAGMENTS AND RAYS

Crookes was able to show that the bands were caused by something moving from the negative electrode (the cathode) toward the positive electrode (the anode). He gave the name "cathode rays" to these streams of mysterious objects.

Another English physicist, J. J. Thomson, applied electric and magnetic fields to cathode rays. He was able to show that they consisted of identical, negatively charged particles. Furthermore, they were the same no matter what sort of gas was in the tube, and they seemed to be much lighter than even the lightest atom. Thomson claimed that these particles were all fragments of atoms. They were soon named "electrons" from the Greek word *elektron*, which means "amber" (static electricity was first made by rubbing amber).

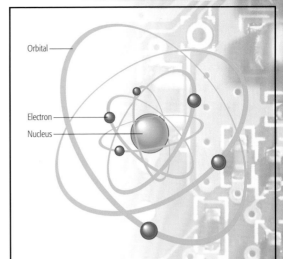

Orbital

Electron

Nucleus

ELECTRONS IN ORBITALS

In an atom the negatively charged electrons surround the positively charged nucleus. The regions in which they are found are known as orbitals. Shown here is an atom of carbon, with its six electrons.

J. J. THOMSON

Joseph John Thomson was born in the northern English city of Manchester in 1856. After studying at the universities of Manchester and Cambridge, he became a professor of experimental physics at Cambridge. For discovering electrons Thomson was awarded the 1906 Nobel Prize in Physics, and he received a knighthood in 1908. He suggested the "plum-pudding" theory of the structure of the atom. According to this theory, in each atom the negatively charged electrons float in a cloud of positive charge, like the pieces of fruit in a plum pudding. Although this idea was shown to be wrong by Ernest Rutherford's work, Thomson went on to make other important discoveries. In 1912 he found that the gas neon occurs in two chemically identical forms, or "isotopes." It turned out that most elements have two or more isotopes. Thomson died in 1940.

Cathode rays consist of electrons that have emerged at the cathode, and flow from the cathode toward the anode. They collide with gas atoms on the way, knocking further electrons out of those atoms.

If the normally electrically neutral atom contains negatively charged electrons, it had to contain equal amounts of balancing positive charge. So how were the electrons and the positive charge arranged in the atom?

A POSITIVE CORE

A New Zealand-born physicist, Ernest Rutherford, probed deeper into the atom in 1911. For this he used alpha particles, which are given out in radioactivity. They are helium atoms that have lost their electrons and are thus positively charged. Rutherford allowed them to strike a thin sheet of gold. Most went right through, but a tiny number were deflected, some of them quite strongly.

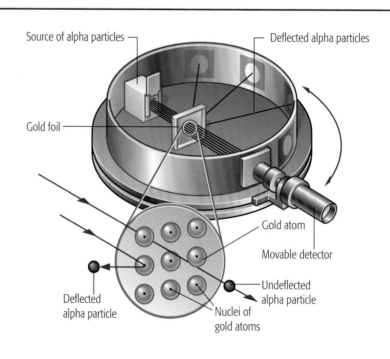

Source of alpha particles

Deflected alpha particles

Gold foil

Gold atom

Movable detector

Deflected alpha particle

Nuclei of gold atoms

Undeflected alpha particle

The Heart of the Atom

Ernest Rutherford allowed positively charged alpha particles to bombard a thin foil of gold. Most passed straight through, but a small number of the particles were deflected through large angles, showing they had bounced off a positively charged core, or nucleus, within the atom.

The only way Rutherford could explain this was to suppose that the positive charge was concentrated in a tiny core, or nucleus (plural nuclei), at the center of the atom. Most alpha particles missed the nuclei but some came very close, felt a powerful force of repulsion, and bounced back.

The nucleus proved to have one ten-thousandth the diameter of the atom. Electrons roam through the outer parts of the atom—relatively speaking, a truly enormous volume.

Ernest Rutherford, seen here, is often called the father of nuclear physics. The chemical element rutherfordium was named for him.

CHAPTER TWO

EXPERIMENTING WITH ELECTRONS

Ingenious experiments revealed the properties of electrons. They proved to be responsible for the most significant properties of all of the matter around us. When they break loose from their atoms, electrons can flow as electric currents.

William Crookes carried out experiments with his tube which showed that cathode rays consist of something moving from the cathode to the anode. He was able to demonstrate that these objects could exert pressure on obstacles placed in their path. Also, J. J. Thomson had shown that the objects were probably very small.

The American physicist Robert Millikan, who measured the charge on the electron in 1909, confirmed these

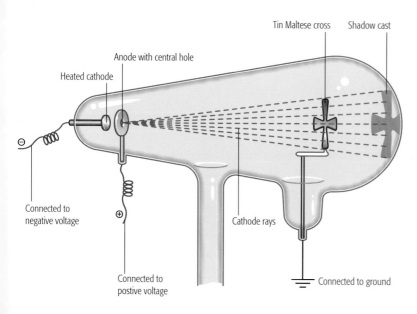

Tin Maltese cross

Shadow cast

Anode with central hole

Heated cathode

Connected to negative voltage

Cathode rays

Connected to positive voltage

Connected to ground

THE CROOKES TUBE

An air pump reduces the pressure in the glass tube. When a high voltage is applied between the two electrodes (cathode and anode), negatively charged particles move from the cathode (negative electrode) toward the anode (positive electrode). These "cathode rays" overshoot and strike the far end of the tube, making it glow. They cast a shadow if an obstacle is put in their path. (Crookes himself used a thin piece of tin in the shape of a Maltese cross.)

facts. When combined with earlier measurements by Thomson, this showed that the mass of the electron was approximately one two-thousandth of the mass of a hydrogen atom.

Physicists now understood what electric currents were. They consist of electrons that have broken free from their atoms and are drifting through, say, a metal wire, or sometimes through space, like the streams of electrons in the Crookes tube. Currents generate heat as the electrons bump into atoms. If they generate enough heat, the temperature of the material rises until it glows—this is what happens in the tungsten filament in an electric lightbulb.

MOVING IN ORBIT

The experiments by Ernest Rutherford (see pages 8–9) had shown that the outer regions of atoms were occupied by electrons, while at the center was the nucleus, positively charged and carrying most of the atom's mass. It was natural to think of the atom as being like a miniature solar system, with the electrons playing the role of planets and orbiting the central nucleus, which stood for the Sun. The electrons were held in place not by gravity but by the attraction between

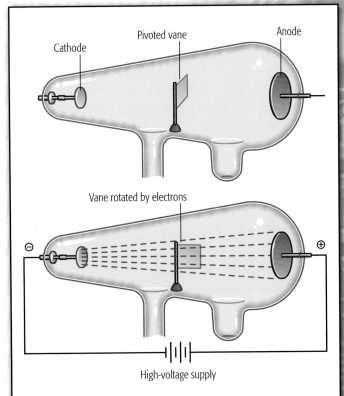

Cathode   Pivoted vane   Anode

Vane rotated by electrons

High-voltage supply

PRESSURE OF ELECTRONS

In one of the demonstrations that can be carried out with a Crookes tube, a vane that is free to rotate is placed inside it. When a voltage is applied, the vane is pushed around until it is parallel with the stream of cathode rays. This confirms that cathode rays are particles rather than waves.

their negative charges and the positive charge on the nucleus.

There was a huge problem with this picture. According to the theories that existed, electrons whirling around within the atom like this should give out all their energy in a brief burst of electromagnetic radiation as they spiraled into the

WILLIAM CROOKES

By the time Sir William Crookes died in 1919, one of his greatest contributions to science, the Crookes tube, had already been used to create crude images. But he could hardly have dreamed that within a few years of his death it was to become the basis for a whole new technology of communication: television. However, the great scientific importance of the Crookes tube had earned him a knighthood, awarded in 1897. The tube was also used as one of the earliest sources of X-rays. Crookes, born in 1832, was a highly practical person and invented improved methods of making sugar from beet, dyeing textiles, and extracting silver and gold from their ores. He also invented several scientific instruments and publicized the benefits of electric lighting. In 1861 he discovered the metal thallium from the new and unknown pattern of colors in its spectrum and went on to study it.

nucleus. All atoms should collapse within a fraction of a second.

The Danish physicist Niels Bohr suggested in 1912 that electrons can occupy only certain orbits, each orbit having its own definite amount of energy. The only way they can move between orbits is to make an abrupt jump from one to another, giving out or taking in energy, in the form of electromagnetic radiation, in amounts corresponding to the differences in the energy levels of the orbits. Atoms do not collapse because their lowest energy levels are filled with electrons. From this picture of the atom was gradually developed quantum theory, which is the basis of modern physics.

One theory was that the atom was structured like the solar system, with electrons moving in orbit around the nucleus just as planets orbit around the Sun.

The Crookes tube and the discovery of cathode rays led to the development of the cathode ray tube, which was used to create images in early television sets.

CHAPTER THREE

THE AGE OF ELECTRONICS

By the beginning of the 20th century electricity had long been doing useful work in several industries. Soon devices called vacuum tubes offered new ways of controlling the flow of electrons. They ushered in the electronics age.

Before long the Crookes tube was developed from a scientific instrument into a practical tool. Many types of "vacuum tube" (they actually contained a low-pressure gas) were devised for different tasks.

The simplest vacuum tube is called a diode and contains two electrodes—a cathode and an anode. The cathode is heated, making it give off electrons. When the anode is at a positive voltage in relation to the cathode, it attracts the electrons. When the anode is at a negative voltage in relation to the cathode, electrons cannot flow to it. Being cold, the anode does not give off electrons, so electrons cannot flow from the anode to the cathode. As far as current flow is concerned, a diode is a one-way device, called a rectifier.

Rectifiers are important devices in electronics. Power is normally supplied with an alternating (reversing)

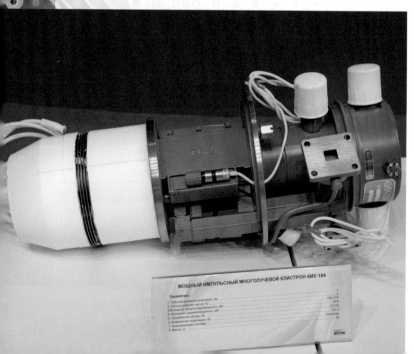

Klystron tubes (known simply as klystrons) are needed to produce the high-power, high-frequency waves used in radar sets.

current, or AC, but there is often a need to turn AC into direct current (DC). That is when a rectifier is needed.

AMPLIFICATION

Currents often need to be amplified, or increased in strength. For example, in a radio the weak current, called the signal, from the antenna must be strengthened to drive the loudspeaker. The pattern of waves in the signal must be copied exactly.

A triode can carry out the job of amplifying. The triode is a vacuum tube with a third electrode called a grid. The grid is a metal mesh surrounding the cathode. A separate small negative voltage applied to the grid holds back the electrons so that fewer of them pass through the grid. The small changes in the signal voltage produce large changes in the current reaching the anode.

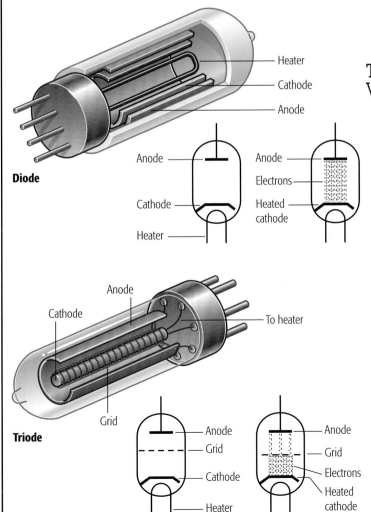

Diode

Heater
Cathode
Anode

Anode
Cathode
Heater

Anode
Electrons
Heated cathode

Triode

Anode
Cathode
Grid
To heater

Anode
Grid
Cathode
Heater

Anode
Grid
Electrons
Heated cathode

TWO KINDS OF VACUUM TUBE

A diode contains a heated cathode, or electron-emitter, and an anode, or electron-receiver. In a triode a third electrode, called a grid, controls the flow of electrons. The left-hand schematic symbols show how the diode and triode are represented in circuit diagrams.

OSCILLOSCOPES

Another development of the vacuum tube turned into a major scientific instrument. In the oscilloscope electrons from a heated cathode called an electron gun are focused by electric and magnetic fields into a narrow beam. The beam is aimed at one end of the tube, which is shaped to form a circular screen and is coated on the inside with a substance called a phosphor. When the beam strikes the phosphor, it produces a glowing dot of light. The beam makes a "pencil" that can be scanned across the screen extremely quickly to trace a graph showing rapidly changing signals.

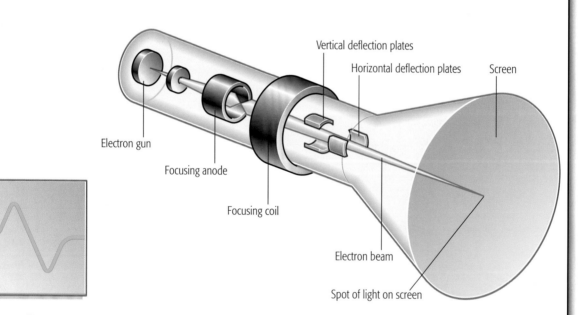

Vertical deflection plates

Horizontal deflection plates

Screen

Electron gun

Focusing anode

Focusing coil

Electron beam

Spot of light on screen

Cathode-Ray Tube

In a cathode-ray tube electrons are focused to form a dot on the screen. The beam is repeatedly swept from side to side and up and down to trace a graph showing measurements of, for example, a nerve signal (above left).

The development of the triode made telephone communications over long distances possible.

CHAPTER FOUR

VACUUM TUBES IN ACTION

Vacuum tubes were once used in almost all electronic equipment. Some were more complex than the diode and triode, and tubes containing eight or more electrodes were designed. Vacuum tubes are still important, particularly in the form of cathode-ray tubes, which are used to generate images in some TVs and computer monitors.

Today, transistors and other solid-state devices have largely taken the place of vacuum tubes. But some of the applications in which they are still used are very important.

One major use of vacuum tubes today is to generate X-rays (see chapter five). Another use is for the picture tubes of television sets and computer VDUs (video display units). Similar screens provide the radar displays that are used by navigators and air-traffic controllers.

Oscilloscopes were once used in many medical procedures. Today, many medical imaging devices produce digital images instead.

USING DIODES

The main use of diodes is to convert alternating current (AC) to direct current (DC). A diode passes current in one direction only. When an alternating voltage (left, red) is applied to it, a one-way voltage (right, blue) is developed.

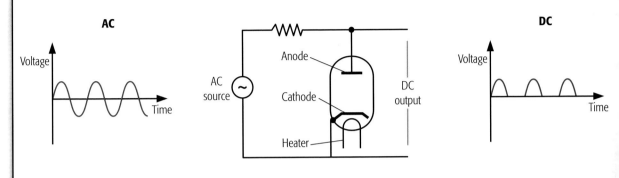

PRACTICAL USES

Oscilloscopes are used in many scientific and industrial instruments. Physicians monitor the body processes of patients with instruments such as the electrocardiograph (for the heart) and electroencephalograph (for the brain).

However, vacuum tubes are starting to be replaced by flat screens that use solid-state devices. At present they are used primarily for very compact displays, such as those on laptop computers. As they are improved, however, they will gradually replace bulky picture tubes.

Vacuum tubes have special uses in industry and military activity. Very powerful amplifiers for large currents still use vacuum tubes rather than solid-state devices. And some rock musicians think traditional amplifiers give a better sound than ones based on transistors. Some key military equipment uses vacuum tubes because they cannot be knocked out by a

LEE DE FOREST

Electronics was revolutionized when the U.S. inventor Lee De Forest invented the triode in 1906. The triode made it possible to use radio waves to broadcast sound and not just the dots and dashes of Morse code. Just four years later De Forest, who was born in 1873, made the first broadcast of an opera. While his triode tube became fundamental to all electronics, De Forest continued to innovate. Among his many other inventions were methods of recording sound on movie film and for television. He died in 1961.

pulse of electromagnetic radiation, which can destroy solid-state devices.

High-power radio transmitters use large vacuum tubes to generate carrier waves. These waves are continuous transmissions that are modulated (varied) by the radio signals being broadcast. The tubes operate at various wavelengths, from short wave to long wave. Other vacuum devices produce microwaves for use in radio communications and radar. Chief among them is the klystron, which is generally made of metal. Its uses range from domestic microwave ovens to continuous-beam radar systems. Klystron tubes can also be used as microwave amplifiers. The magnetron is a similar type of vacuum tube that is favored for very high-power pulsed radar systems.

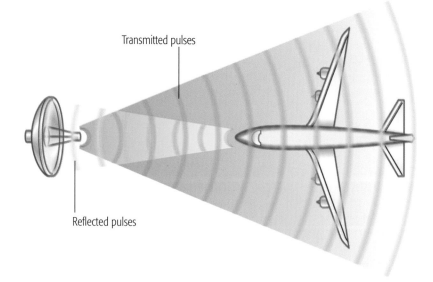

Transmitted pulses

Reflected pulses

SEEING WITHOUT LIGHT

Vacuum tubes are used in generating radar waves. Transmitted in directional beams from equipment on the ground, pulses of radar waves are reflected from objects such as an airplane and are collected and focused, often by the same dish from which they were sent.

Oscilloscopes are often used to test and repair electronic equipment.

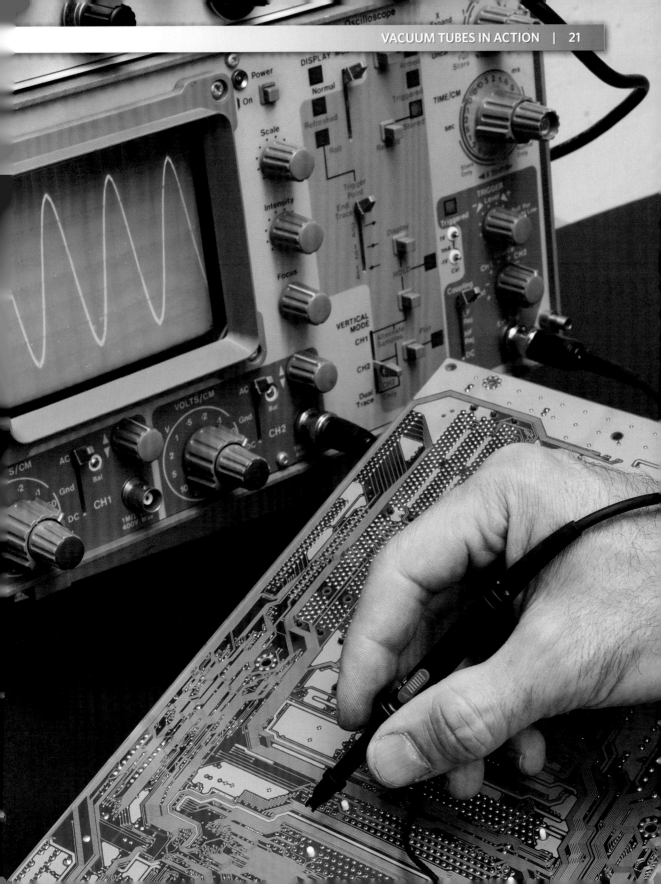

CHAPTER FIVE

X-RAY VISION

With X-rays physicians can iden-tify disease and injury in the human body, engineers can detect flaws in industrial components, *and customs officials can discover smuggled goods and danger-ous weapons hidden in baggage. Beyond X-rays are gamma rays.*

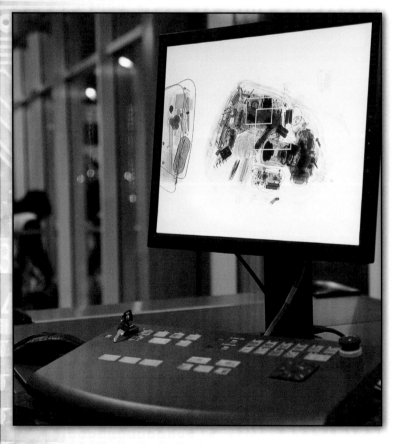

The German physi-cist Wilhelm Roentgen noticed in 1897 that while he was generating cathode rays in a Crookes tube, a screen that was covered with a barium com-pound began to glow, even though the tube had been placed inside a cardboard box. His

The contents of a suitcase are revealed in this X-ray image created at an air-port security checkpoint. Experienced TSA and cus-toms officials can recognize suspicious features in a complex image like this.

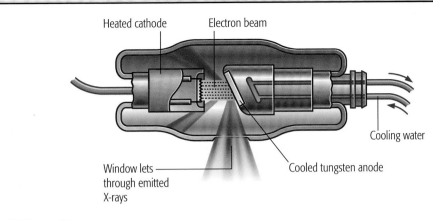

Heated cathode

Electron beam

Cooling water

Cooled tungsten anode

Window lets through emitted X-rays

X-RAY TUBE

A high-speed beam of electrons striking a tungsten plate, which has to be cooled to prevent it from melting, generates X-rays.

experiments showed that the tube was sending out a highly penetrating, short-wavelength radiation, which he called X-rays (the "X" representing "unknown"). It was found that X-rays could be used to take photographs of normally invisible things such as the bones of living people.

X-rays are electromagnetic radiation, differing from visible light only in their short wavelengths. X-rays have a much higher energy than visible light. An X-ray is given out when an electron jumps from one energy level in the atom to a deeper one with a much lower energy. This happens when electrons bombard matter and knock other electrons out of the innermost orbits of some atoms.

What happens then is that electrons from higher orbits jump into the spaces created in these lower orbits, losing energy that is given out as X-rays.

BEYOND X-RAYS

Beyond the highest-energy X-rays are gamma rays, which are given off in radioactive processes. Gamma rays generally come from the nucleus, and electrons play no part in producing them. However, another important process that produces gamma rays is the annihilation of an electron with its antiparticle, a positron. A positron has the same mass as an electron but in every other way is its opposite. It

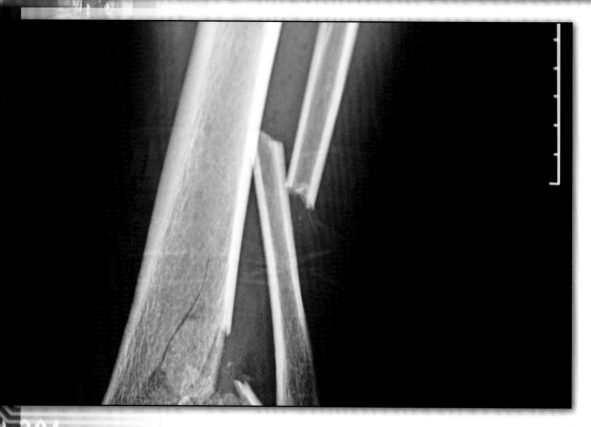

This medical X-ray machine "sees" through a person's skin and flesh to reveal a broken bone in the leg.

has a positive charge equal to the negative charge of the electron, and it has opposite magnetic properties. Positrons are rare. When one is produced in a nuclear process, it soon collides with an electron, and the two disappear completely, being converted into two gamma rays.

X-RAY ASTRONOMY

X-rays and gamma rays are important to astronomers. They are emitted by high-energy sources such as very hot stars and the centers of some galaxies. Studying these radiations tells us more about these objects than we can learn from just the visible light they give out. Special detectors have to be launched on orbiting observatories because gamma rays and X-rays are absorbed by the Earth's atmosphere. Various detectors are used, some of which convert the radiation into visible light.

Images of this star cluster, located about 6,500 light years from Earth, were taken with the Chandra X-Ray Observatory, a space telescope launched by NASA in 1999.

CHAPTER SIX

UNDERSTANDING SEMICONDUCTORS

The compact and powerful computers, radios, TV sets, and other electronics goods that surround us are solid-state devices. This means that instead of tubes, they are based on solid crystalline materials called semiconductors. The special properties of semiconductors arise from the behavior of the electrons in their atoms.

Electrically, materials fall into three main groups: conductors, insulators, and semiconductors. The revolutionary change away from vacuum tubes was

John Bardeen, William Shockley, and Walter Brattain developed the transistor while working at Bell Labs, which was, at the time, part of the AT&T Corporation.

made possible by semiconductors.

In a conductor, such as a metal, more current flows if a greater voltage is applied to it. There are always huge numbers of free electrons in the metal that have been separated from their atoms. In an insulating material, such as rubber or many kinds of plastic, there are very few free electrons, and large voltages can be applied to them without large currents flowing.

Semiconducting materials, such as the elements germanium, silicon, and gallium, have very few free electrons at low temperatures, but more as the temperature increases. A temperature increase means more vibration of the atoms, and this "shakes" electrons free of some of the atoms. Shining light onto some semiconductors also "shakes" more electrons free.

The different energy levels in which electrons are arranged in atoms are known as shells. Each shell can hold only a certain number of electrons. The innermost shell holds two, and the next holds eight. The third shell can be "satisfied" with either eight or 18 electrons—it does not strongly tend to lose or gain electrons when it has either of these numbers. Atoms become more stable by losing or gaining electrons so that they have only filled shells. This explains the ways in which atoms combine with one another— they either lose or gain electrons, or share them, to achieve filled shells.

Elements that are good electrical conductors, such as metals, can easily lose their outermost electrons, which form a "sea" throughout the material and are easily set in motion when a voltage is applied.

Silicon, with 14 electrons in its atom, has the first two shells filled, but has only four electrons in the outermost shell. However, silicon atoms can share electrons with one another. In a silicon crystal

BARDEEN, BRATTAIN, AND SHOCKLEY

The transistor that was to replace the vacuum tube and revolutionize electronics was the brainchild of three brilliant researchers working at the Bell Telephone Laboratories. Walter Brattain was born in 1902 and raised on a cattle ranch. John Bardeen had worked as a geophysicist before joining Bell. William Shockley, born in 1910, had directed research into antisubmarine warfare during World War II. The three men first devised a type of transistor known as the point-contact transistor, using a germanium crystal. Then Shockley invented the junction transistor, which was to become the most widely used type of transistor. The three of them shared the 1956 Nobel Prize in Physics. Shockley went on to head his own Shockley Transistor Corporation. Bardeen became a professor at Illinois University and in 1972 shared another Nobel Prize in Physics. He had developed, with Leon Cooper and John Schrieffer, the BCS theory (named from their initials) that explained what causes superconductivity. Superconductivity is the loss of electrical resistance by some materials that occurs at very low temperatures.

each atom has four neighbors. By sharing its electrons with these neighbors, an atom effectively has eight electrons in its third shell. At low temperatures such shared electrons are tightly bound in place and cannot flow.

However, at higher temperatures some of the electrons are sometimes jiggled out of place. If a voltage is applied, they can move and form a current. These mobile electrons are called charge carriers. This difference in electrical behavior at different temperatures is what makes scientists class silicon as a semiconductor.

ADDING IMPURITIES

Adding a very small proportion of impurities consisting of atoms of a different type can increase the number of charge carriers. An example is arsenic, which has 33 electrons. Of them 28 fill the first three shells (2 + 8 + 18), and five lie in the outermost shell. A few arsenic atoms can be fitted into the crystalline array of silicon atoms. They share four of their electrons with electrons from four neighboring atoms, but one is left over, and it can go wandering for large distances through the crystal. The arsenic atom left behind is now positively charged and is called an ion. It is fixed in place. The mobile charge carriers are negatively charged electrons. This sort of semiconductor is called *n*-type ("n" for negative).

Aluminum is an example of another type of impurity atom. Each of its atoms has 13 electrons, with 10 in the first two shells and three in the outermost shell. If aluminum atoms are added to the silicon lattice, they can share electrons with

Single-crystal, or monocrystalline, silicon is grown in the shape of cylinders, like this. The cylinder is then cut into thin slices.

three neighbors, but each atom will be one electron short of a filled shell. This gap is called a "hole."

Occasionally a nearby electron may jump into such a hole, and then a positively charged hole is left at the point from which the electron came.

It is just as if the hole had jumped in the opposite direction. If a voltage is then applied across the silicon crystal, electrons will move in one direction. Those that are near holes jump into them, leaving holes behind. Other electrons jump into those holes, and so on. In this way electrons move across the crystal in one direction, while positively charged holes appear to move in the opposite direction.

Engineers view this silicon "doped" with aluminum as being filled with mobile positive holes. (There is also a small proportion of mobile electrons, freed from their parent atoms by thermal vibrations, but it is holes that dominate. Similarly, in *n*-type material, although electrons dominate, there are a few holes present.) Material in which charge is mostly carried by holes is called *p*-type ("p" for positive). When a hole moves a long way, what really happens is that many electrons each hop a short distance from one atom to a neighboring one.

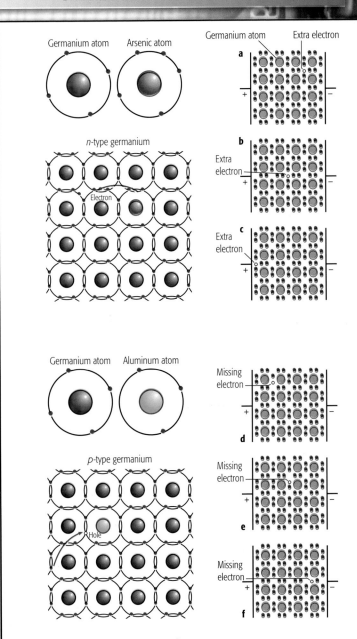

N-TYPE AND P-TYPE SEMICONDUCTORS

An arsenic impurity atom in a lattice of germanium atoms has an extra electron (top left). Such electrons wander through the lattice, making it an *n*-type semiconductor. An aluminum atom has an electron missing from its outermost shell, creating a "hole" that wanders around like a positive charge (bottom left), making it a *p*-type semiconductor. When an electric field is applied to the semiconductor (a, d), electrons move toward the positive terminal (b, c), but holes drift toward the negative terminal (e, f).

BIRTH OF THE TRANSISTOR

Scientists had known of the existence of semiconductors since the late 19th century, but it was only in the 1940s that three researchers at the Bell Telephone Laboratories in New Jersey discovered how to use them in devices that would do the job of vacuum tubes. The first transistor, a tiny device, could do the job of a bulky triode: it could amplify a voltage. That is to say, if a weak varying signal voltage was applied to it, a larger voltage was generated that had the same wave pattern.

Its small size was not the only advantage that the transistor (the word is an abbreviation of "transfer resistor") had

This is a replica of the first working transistor, created in 1948. It is about 1 centimeter (0.4 in.) tall. The electrical connections to the emitter, base, and collector can be seen. The transistors that went into commercial production a few years later were smaller and more neatly packaged than this.

over the vacuum tube. It did not need to be heated, so it used much less energy than a vacuum tube. It was also more reliable.

The first design was soon improved, and within a few years commercial products containing semiconductor devices began to appear. It was not only triodes and other amplifier devices that were replaced. Vacuum-tube diodes were also replaced by semiconductor diodes. Computers, radios, and TV sets all became "transistorized."

The small size of the transistor allowed devices such as radios to become small enough for people to easily carry anywhere.

CHAPTER SEVEN

FORWARD AND REVERSE BIAS

Since the invention of the prototype transistor in 1948 a huge number of different types have been developed. Each type is designed to serve a certain specialized purpose. All depend on the fact that in semiconductors electric current is carried by two sorts of charge—negative electrons and positive holes.

A solid-state diode consists of a piece of *p*-type semiconductor in close contact with a piece of *n*-type semiconductor. For example, one kind of diode is made by taking a piece of *p*-type material and adding impurity atoms to a small region to turn that part into *n*-type material. The boundary between the two types of material is called a junction. Alternatively, a small region of *p*-type material can be created within a piece of *n*-type material by adding impurity atoms of a different kind.

FORWARD BIASING

Suppose that the *p*-type material is connected to the positive terminal of a battery, and the *n*-type material is connected to the negative terminal (as in the first illustration in the second row on the right). This is called foward-biasing the diode. The battery pushes a stream of electrons into the *n*-type material. The electrons in the *n*-type material are therefore forced

LEDs (light-emitting diodes) are ideal for use wherever a low-power indicator light is needed.

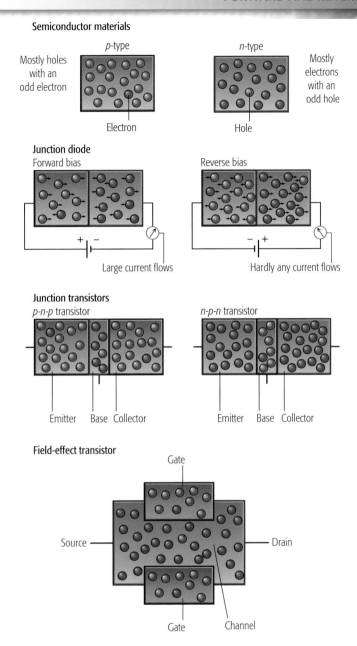

Semiconductor materials

p-type

Mostly holes
with an
odd electron

Electron

n-type

Mostly
electrons
with an
odd hole

Hole

Junction diode

Forward bias

Reverse bias

+ −

Large current flows

− +

Hardly any current flows

Junction transistors

p-n-p transistor

Emitter   Base   Collector

n-p-n transistor

Emitter   Base   Collector

Field-effect transistor

Gate

Source

Drain

Gate   Channel

SOLID-STATE DIODES AND TRANSISTORS

A solid-state junction diode consists of a piece of p-type material and a piece of n-type material joined together. Current can flow only one way across the junction. In the junction transistor a piece of one type of material, called the base, is sandwiched between two pieces of the other kind. In the field-effect transistor the job of the base is done by the gate, consisting of one type of material (p-type is shown here) that has been diffused into a larger piece of material of the opposite type.

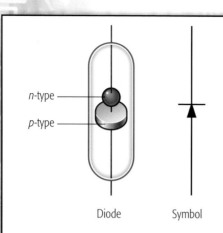
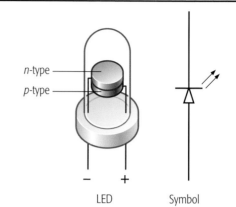

Diode   Symbol   LED   Symbol

DIODES

Current can flow only one way through a diode. The arrowhead in the circuit symbol shows the direction of movement of positive current. A light-emitting diode (LED) is made of materials that give out light when a current flows through them.

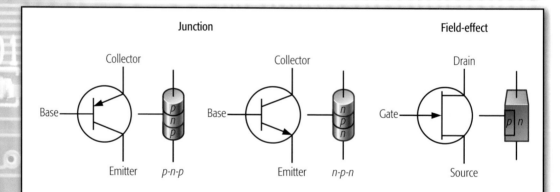

Junction   Field-effect

Collector   Collector   Drain

Base   Base   Gate

Emitter   *p-n-p*   Emitter   *n-p-n*   Source

TRANSISTORS

In junction transistors (left and center) changes in base voltage control the flow of electrons from emitter to collector. In the field-effect transistor (right) the gate voltage controls the flow of electrons from source to drain.

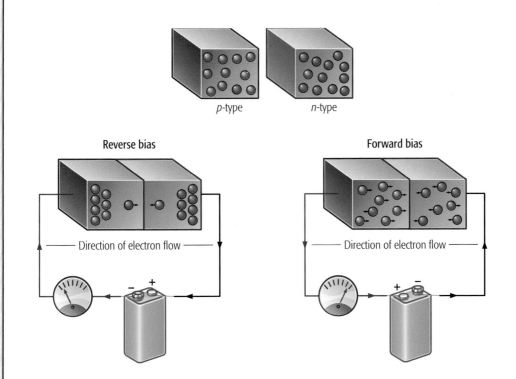

BIASING A SEMICONDUCTOR JUNCTION

Reverse bias (left): charge carriers are pulled away from the junction but can then go no farther. Forward bias (right): there is a steady flow of holes and electrons toward the junction, where they neutralize each other.

toward the junction. At the same time, the positive terminal attracts electrons out of the p-type material of the diode. This creates holes that are filled by electrons coming from deeper within the material. It is as though holes are flowing toward the junction—which just means from the junction.

Holes and electrons meet at the junction and neutralize each other. The positive and negative charges cancel, so that there is no charge overall at that point. As a result, current flows freely when the diode is forward-biased.

REVERSE BIASING

If the connections to the battery are reversed (second illustration, second row on page 33), the battery tries to draw charge carriers away from the junction.

In n-type material, when electrons are pulled away from the junction, they are not replaced. The p-type material on the other side of the junction cannot supply replacement electrons. As the negatively charged electrons are removed, they leave a region of positive charge behind. This attracts the electrons and eventually stops them from being pulled any farther.

In the p-type material the holes are also pulled away from the junction a little way and then stop. As a result, no current can flow through a reverse-biased diode. The fact that current can flow only one way makes the diode ideal as a rectifier in radios and many other devices.

JUNCTION TRANSISTORS

The junction transistor consists of three types of semiconductor joined together (see the third row in the illustration on page 33)—either p-type material sandwiched between two pieces of n-type material (called an n-p-n transistor), or n-type material sandwiched between p-type pieces (a p-n-p transistor). Or the transistor can be made from a single piece of semiconductor containing different p-type and n-type regions. The central section is called the base, while the two ends are called the emitter and the collector.

The junction transistor is like two semiconductor diodes back to back. Take an n-p-n transistor as an example: If a small positive voltage is applied to the p-type base, the emitter/base junction is forward-biased. Holes flow from the p-type base into the emitter, and electrons flow from the n-type emitter into the base.

A larger positive voltage is applied to the collector. Many of the electrons entering the base reach the junction between the base and the collector. The base is made thin to help them do this. The electrons are attracted across the junction and into the collector, and from there they pass into the external circuit.

So, a small base current, consisting of electrons flowing out of the base, results in a large collector current, consisting of electrons flowing out of the collector. Thus the transistor acts as an amplifying device.

FIELD-EFFECT TRANSISTOR

The field-effect transistor, or FET (see the lower illustration on page 33), consists of a piece of n-type material called the channel. There is a p-type region, called the gate, on each side of it. When a positive voltage is applied to the right end, electrons flow into the device at the left end (called the source) and leave at the right end (called the drain).

If a negative voltage is applied to the gates, the gate/channel junctions are reverse-biased. No electrons can flow into the gates because of the reverse bias. The effect of the negative voltage also extends into the channel and reduces the flow of electrons from source to drain. If the gates' negative voltage is increased, the current in the channel decreases still more.

So, in the FET small changes in the gate voltage cause large changes in the current that flows through the device, and thus the FET can be used to amplify signals.

A modern transistor is tiny compared with a person's fingertip. The device itself is inside the protective packaging. Three metal connectors emerge, coming from the emitter, base, and collector. They are easily inserted into a circuit board.

CHAPTER EIGHT

BUILDING MICROCHIPS

Microchips are literally chips of semiconductor, carrying electronic circuits of quite staggering complexity. Manufactured in batches of hundreds at a time, they are plentiful and cheap, providing the computing power in "smart" devices all around us.

Miniaturization of electronic devices began with the development of printed circuit boards, known as PCBs. A PCB is made from a single piece of copper foil attached to a plastic base. The parts of the copper that are not needed are etched away with acids. What remains after this is a network of copper pathways that provide the connections between components that will be added, completing the circuit.

In almost any electronic device there is at least one PCB, with a host of components mounted onto it and soldered to it. The PCB is compact, convenient to handle, and easy to manufacture in large numbers with complete accuracy—and therefore it is cheap.

The size of the ant in this picture shows the size of the microchip that it is gripping. The standard size of a chip is 6 mm (1/4 in.) square.

PRINTED CIRCUITS

A printed circuit gets its name because an essential part of its manufacture involves printing the circuit design onto the board. This design then remains while the copper in other areas is etched away (see the box). The same principle is used in making integrated circuits. An integrated circuit consists of various electronic components formed in a single piece of semiconductor material.

MAKING CHIPS

A microchip is made from a rod of very pure crystalline semiconductor. The following description applies to silicon, the most commonly used material. It is manufactured so that there is less than one unwanted impurity atom in 1 billion. But there are controlled amounts of a desired impurity, such as boron or indium, which is what makes the silicon into *p*-type material.

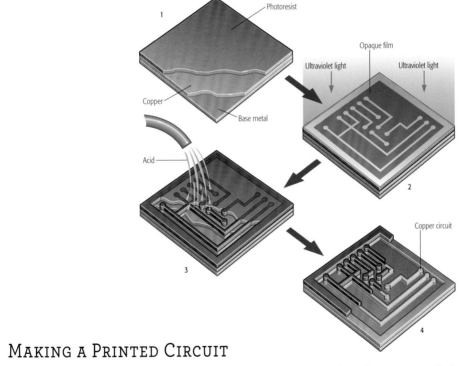

MAKING A PRINTED CIRCUIT

(1) A nonconducting base material (brown) is coated with copper and then with photoresist (blue). (2) An opaque film carrying the transparent circuit design is placed on this and illuminated with ultraviolet light (green). The parts exposed to light are "hardened." (3) Acids remove the unexposed photoresist and the copper areas beneath. The circuit stays intact. (4) The areas of hardened photoresist are removed, leaving the copper circuit.

MAKING A MICROCHIP

1

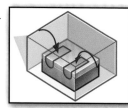

A *p*-type silicon wafer is baked in an oxidation oven to 1,000°C (1,830°F), which produces a thin protective layer of silicon dioxide on the surface.

2

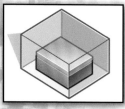

A light-sensitive coating called photoresist is applied to the silicon dioxide layer, and over it is laid a film mask of the circuit design. Ultraviolet light is shined through the mask.

3

The mask is removed, and the wafer is treated with a developer that removes the areas of photoresist not exposed to ultraviolet light. These are the areas that represent circuit components.

4

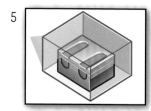

Hydrofluoric acid etches away the silicon dioxide in the areas where photoresist has been removed. Then the remainder of the photoresist is removed, and the wafer is exposed to phosphorus vapor in an oven. Phosphorus atoms diffuse into the silicon, creating *n*-type regions where the silicon dioxide has been removed.

5

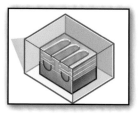

The wafer is returned to the oxidation oven, where another layer of silicon dioxide is added in preparation for further stages of etching.

6

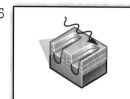

The wafer is given another coating of photoresist, and further masking and etching stages are carried out.

7

The wafer is returned to the oxidation oven to add another layer of silicon dioxide.

8

The next stages of masking and etching make the channels previously created deeper and narrower.

9

The wafer is placed in a vacuum chamber and exposed to aluminum vapor. A layer of aluminum is added to the wafer.

10

The wafer goes through a final series of masking and etching stages that form the electrical connections for the complete circuit.

Electronic devices normally incorporate a large number of integrated circuits. Here an array of microchips is attached to a circuit board. Each chip is mounted in a plastic package from which metal pins protrude. The pins are plugged into a printed circuit board to make the necessary electrical connections.

A thin circular disk approximately 5 centimeters (2 inches) across is cut from the rod and polished to form a perfectly flat wafer about a fifth of a millimeter (1/125 inch) thick. Hundreds of microchips can be made from a single wafer.

The *p*-type material will form the underlying substrate of the microchips, an inactive supporting layer. Areas of *n*-type material are formed in the upper part of the substrate, each one the starting point of a component such as a transistor or a diode.

When the finished component is used, a negative voltage is connected to the *p*-type material, which means it is reverse-biased in relation to the regions of *n*-type material. This also means that no current can flow from each component into the substrate, and so they are all well insulated from one another.

The sequence on the opposite page shows the production of part of a single circuit, starting with a piece of *p*-type silicon. Hundreds of identical microcircuits are made simultaneously in several layers within a single wafer of semiconductor.

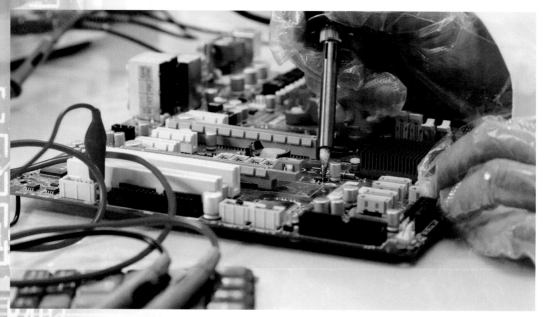

Soldering irons and soldering guns are used to assemble and repair electronic components. Too much heat from the tool, however, can damage sensitive microchips.

COATINGS AND MASKS

The wafer is put into an oxidation oven where atoms of oxygen combine with the silicon in the upper layer of the wafer, about half a micrometer (about 20 millionths of an inch) thick. This is coated with a material called photoresist.

Then a film called a mask is placed over the wafer. Most of the film is clear, but the circuit design appears on it as a network of opaque lines. When ultraviolet light is shined onto the mask, it passes through the clear parts and "hardens" the photoresist.

The mask is removed, and acid is applied to etch away the parts of the photoresist that were not exposed to ultraviolet light—that is, the part representing the circuit. The acid also removes the silicon dioxide layer directly beneath, and as a result the circuit pattern is now represented by the exposed surface of p-type silicon.

BUILDING COMPONENTS

The wafer now goes into an oven in which there is a vapor of an element such as phosphorus. The phosphorus atoms diffuse into the exposed areas of the silicon, forming a network of n-type material.

To build up components, more atoms have to be diffused into certain parts of this n-type network. To do this, layers of silicon dioxide and photoresist are again formed on the wafer. A new mask with a different pattern is used to print another network onto the resist, and again unexposed resist and the silicon dioxide layer beneath are removed to expose relevant areas in the surface of the previously created n-type areas.

This time atoms such as boron or indium may be diffused in to create p-type regions, or further doses of phosphorus may be used if higher concentrations of electrons are needed in some parts of the n-type regions.

Finally, the components so created are linked with aluminum connections joined to the upper surfaces of the various n-type and p-type regions in the chip. Some microchips also use electrical connections formed within the semiconductor.

A microprocessor made in this way can contain millions of separate transistors, diodes, capacitors, and resistors in a space of a few square millimeters. The hundreds of such circuits on the wafer are electronically tested, defective ones are marked, and the wafer is broken up and the faulty circuits discarded. Wires are connected at various points to the good chips, and they are mounted in containers, which may be round but are more often rectangular. In most applications the microchip capsules are mounted on a printed circuit board.

The incredibly small size of microchips gives even handheld devices such as smart phones the processing power to perform complex functions.

CHAPTER NINE

DATA STORAGE

Computers work with binary code in which all numbers are represented as a sequence of zeros and ones instead of the ten digits from 0 to 9 that we ordinarily use. A single binary digit, 0 or 1, represents one bit.

A string of eight bits is called a byte and can represent any of 256 different numbers (from 0 to 255). In some contexts the computer treats them as numbers, and in others it treats them as language characters. The 26 letters of the alphabet, both lowercase (small) and upper case (large), punctuation characters, and some other symbols can each be represented by a different byte. The maximum size of a memory is usually expressed in bytes, megabytes (1 MB = 1,048,576 bytes), or gigabytes (1 GB = 1,073,741,824 bytes).

The computer's short-term memory contains data that it is directly working with, including intermediate results in the course of a calculation. This

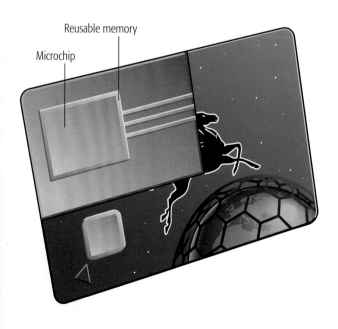

Reusable memory

Microchip

SMART CARD

A smart card is the same size as a normal plastic credit card. But as well as the usual magnetic strip, which records details of the cardholder and the account number, there is a microchip embedded in one corner of the card. The chip has a reusable memory that holds details of purchases and the cardholder's remaining credit.

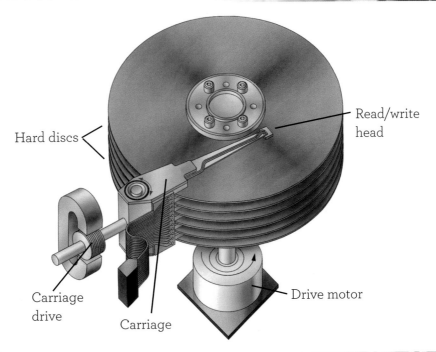

Hard discs

Read/write head

Carriage drive

Carriage

Drive motor

Hard Disc Drive

Backup memory that needs to be accessed rapidly is kept on hard discs. A large memory store consists of a stack of hard discs, mounted on the same spindle and accessed simultaneously. Discs can rotate at speeds of 160 km per hour (100 mph) or more. Data is stored as magnetic fields in areas of the disc as small as 1 micrometer (40 millionths of an inch) across. Read/write heads mounted on the ends of arms swing in and out across each disc as required, "flying" a fraction of a micrometer (a few millionths of an inch) above the disc surface, kept clear of it by a cushion of air. The carriage moves the read/write head in and out.

type of information has to be available immediately, so it is stored in RAM (random-access memory), where any piece of information that is required can be accessed equally quickly. RAM comes in special microchips called RAM chips. The retrieval time from a chip for a single piece of information—known as the access time—can be as little as 5 billionths of a second.

There are two main types of RAM. Dynamic RAM, or DRAM (pronounced "dee-ram"), has to be "refreshed" thousands of times per second—that is, the same data has to be written into it continually. This slows down the rate at which the data can be read or altered, but DRAM is cheap and therefore is the mostly widely used kind of RAM.

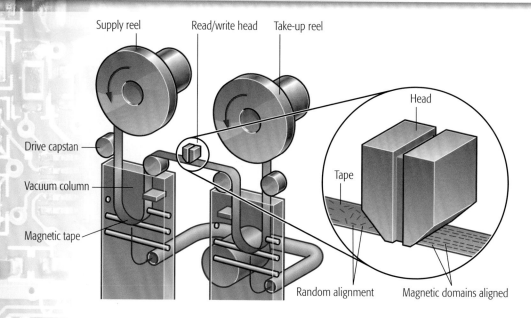

Supply reel   Read/write head   Take-up reel

Head

Drive capstan

Vacuum column

Tape

Magnetic tape

Random alignment   Magnetic domains aligned

TAPE DRIVE

Large computer backup data stores are kept on magnetic tape. The tape is driven past a read/write head by the capstan wheels. The read/write head applies a strong magnetic field that aligns tiny magnetic domains, or regions, in the metal tape coating to represent bits (units of information).

Unlike DRAM, static RAM, or SRAM (pronounced "ess-ram"), does not need to be refreshed. It is more expensive than DRAM, but faster. Both SRAM and DRAM lose their data if the power supply fails.

While a computer is working, the information that is stored in RAM is constantly changing. There is other information that the computer needs, and which does not need to change. It is stored in ROM (read-only memory), which is also random-access memory, but contains data that is not altered. It may contain "boot-up" information, which is used when the computer is first turned on, and other information that is used in the normal running of the computer.

BACKING UP

Data produced by the computer needs to be stored somewhere. The backup or secondary memory needed for this may be provided by magnetic disks. The "floppy" disk, also called a diskette, is a piece of flexible plastic 9 centimeters (3.5 inches) across, coated with a magnetic material. It is contained in a rigid square package made of thicker plastic. The diskette is spun fast while data is recorded on one or both sides. The usual high-density double-sided floppy disk can hold 1.4 MB. Other types of removable disk can hold more.

Hard disk drives provide much higher storage capacities. A drive contains several rigid disks, or platters, mounted on a spindle, and spinning very fast. Magnetic read/write heads, moving as a unit, swing back and forth over each disk, reading the top and bottom sides. The magnetic coating is iron oxide or some other magnetic material. It consists of tiny regions called magnetic domains. Each domain has its own magnetic field. The head's magnetic field rotates the domain fields so that they point one way to represent a 0 or the opposite way to represent a 1. Later the read/write head can read back the data it has recorded by sensing the directions of each of the domain fields.

Even in a home PC a storage capacity of 500 gigabytes or more is now common. (1 gigabyte, or 1 GB, equals 1,024 MB but is often taken to mean 1,000 MB.) A piece of information can be retrieved from the disk in an average time of about a hundredth of a second.

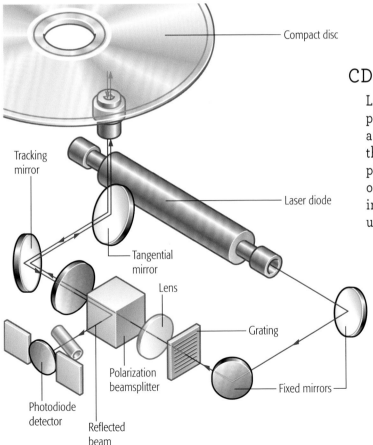

Compact disc

Tracking mirror

Laser diode

Tangential mirror

Lens

Grating

Polarization beamsplitter

Fixed mirrors

Photodiode detector

Reflected beam

CD Drive

Laser light scans the pitted undersurface of a CD. The variations in the reflected beam are picked up by a photodiode detector and turned into sound and images or used as computer data.

A CD-ROM, or CD read-only memory, can store about 700 megabytes of data. One megabyte is over 1 million bytes. CD-ROMs are used for software and for movies and music that can be played back on a computer.

MAGNETIC TAPE

Even larger storage capacity is provided by magnetic tape. The tape stores information in basically the same way as do magnetic disks, audiotapes, and videotapes. (The earliest personal computers used ordinary audiotape cassettes for storage.) However, tape can hold enormous amounts of information.

To access data on a tape, the tape has to be played all the way through to the appropriate point. If a program is to use the data, it must first be copied to a faster medium such as a magnetic disk. For this reason tape is normally used to make secure copies of rarely needed information, such as details of bank customers' past transactions.

CD-ROM

A CD-ROM is a compact disc working in essentially the same way as music CDs. Its name is an abbreviation of "compact disc—read-only memory." It contains information that a computer can read, but in its standard form the information on it cannot be altered.

A CD-ROM consists of an aluminum disc covered with a protective coating of plastic. Tiny pits are etched into the underside of the disc along a track that spirals outward from the center. In the CD-ROM drive a read head bounces a laser beam off the disc as it rotates. At any point along the track there may be a pit, in which case the laser beam is not reflected to the detector, or there may be a "flat," where a pit is missing, in which case the light is reflected to the detector. The sequence of pits and flats causes a fluctuating signal in the detector, which is converted and sent to the computer.

A standard CD-ROM can store about 700 MB of data, which is moderate by today's standards, and it is much slower than a hard disc. However, it is cheap and can safely be removed from a drive and handled—a hard disc is expensive and must not be handled, and most must be kept permanently mounted in an enclosure. Drives that can write to special CDs as well as read them are increasingly common.

The DVD (digital versatile drive) is a compact disc with a higher capacity, measured in gigabytes, and a higher access speed. It is favored for viewing movies because of the extra facilities that a computerized medium offers: It enables quick repeats or skips and can provide other easily accessible extra material, such as background information about the stars, or even alternative "takes" from the movie.

Blu-ray discs, first sold to consumers in 2006, have replaced DVDs in many cases. Each dual-layer disc can hold 50 GB of data.

CHAPTER TEN

SOLID-STATE DEVICES

Electronic devices surround us in everyday life, and nearly all of them are solid-state. Signal lights of all kinds are usually LEDs (light-emitting diodes). Amplifiers are used wherever sounds and images are produced electronically. Manufacturers pack ever more sophisticated miniaturized electronics into cars, motorcycles, and airplanes.

The illuminated digits on a bedside radio/alarm clock, the on-off lights on almost any device, and the sound-level indicators on a music system are nearly always LEDs. They can be made of a choice of semiconductor materials to give out different colors. For example, green is provided by gallium phosphide, and blue by silicon carbide. Infrared LEDs are used in remote controls for TVs and other electronic equipment.

Solid-state amplifiers boost signals from microphones in tape recorders, from antennae in radios and TV sets, from the playback heads in tape and CD players, and from video cameras and video playback machines.

The supercomputers made by Cray Inc. are different from conventional computers in being "massively parallel." Different parts of the computer can work on different parts of a calculation at the same time, while still other parts bring the results together.

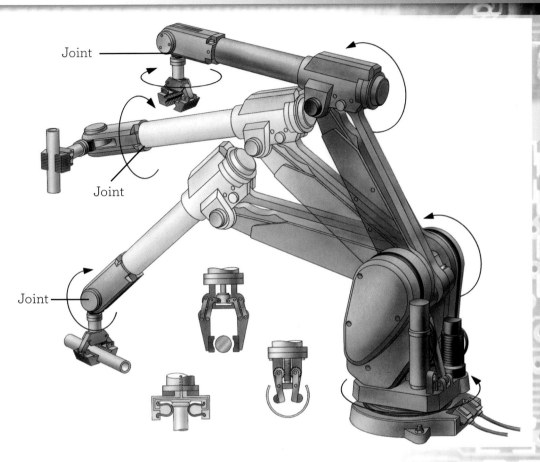

Joint

Joint

Joint

Robot Maneuverability

A robotic arm is jointed in several places, and its fingers can grip objects gently or firmly, as required. Independent motors drive these movements, each controlled by its own microcomputer. The three small illustrations show different attachments for handling objects of different shapes. For example, small tubes can be gripped on the outside, and a U-shaped channel can be gripped on the inside.

SMALL-SCALE COMPUTERS

Small-scale computers are everywhere. When long or complicated sequences of operations need to be performed, engineers often take a microprocessor that is capable of running a computer and adapt it. An example of such a use is seen in the variety of programs (sequences of operations) that ordinary domestic washing machines have built into them.

The ability to put a great deal of computing power just where it is needed is important in the robot arms used on assembly lines in factories. These multi-jointed arms have several built-in motors,

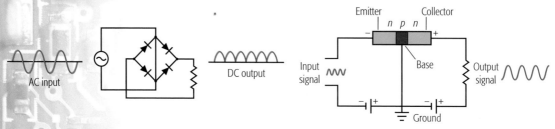

Two Solid-State Circuits

Diodes can be used to make a full-wave rectifier circuit (left), which turns an AC input wave into a DC output. An important use of the transistor is to amplify signals (right).

all of them working independently. An apparently simple action such as reaching out for an object and picking it up requires many interrelated movements of all the arm's joints and precise calculation of the forces needed both to move the heavy arm and to grip an object that may be light or heavy, delicate or tough. The complex computations that are needed are shared between a master computer controlling the whole robot and individual computers controlling each of its motors.

SUPERCOMPUTERS

The abundance of powerful, cheap microcomputers has made possible the development of immensely fast supercomputers. Their architecture, or logical design, is radically different from that of conventional computers. Whereas ordinary computers carry out calculations in a step-by-step process, supercomputers are usually parallel, which means that different parts of a calculation are parceled out to different parts of the machine, all of which are computers in their own right. The results are then combined to yield the final answer. Supercomputers are used for the most complex scientific and technical problems, from forecasting the weather to the creation of special effects in blockbuster movies.

SMART CARS

A driver's ability to make independent decisions is gradually being taken over by electronics. In an automatic-transmission car gear changes are made automatically under the control of sensors that measure the engine's speed and how much force it is having to exert. The mixture of fuel and air delivered to the engine is balanced automatically according to the engine's temperature and the prevailing driving conditions.

When a car skids while braking, its wheels tend to lock. The car's ABS (automatic braking system) can detect this and automatically release and reapply the brakes in rapid succession to regain the braking force. The ABS can also help the driver keep control while braking in a turn.

In today's car a great deal of information is relayed from the car's systems to the driver through the dashboard display. Information about the current trip includes average speed and probable time to the destination. If a problem develops, it may be identified and explained. A warning message may even be flashed if a problem is about to develop.

Electronic systems that are built in as part of a vehicle or other larger device, such as an industrial machine, are described as "embedded." Such embedded systems are also found in racing cars and the most advanced motorcycles.

There is no clear dividing line between embedded electronic systems and the many other electronic systems in the well-equipped modern car that can be regarded as "add-ons." Most new cars have power windows and central locking—that is, door locks controlled by the driver either from the driver's seat or by operating an infrared remote control while he or she leaves or approaches the car.

SMART BIKE

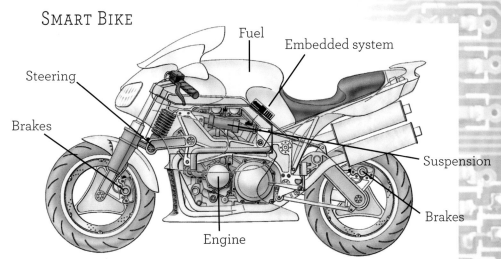

This high-performance motorcycle has a sophisticated "embedded," or built-in, computer system. It can control the fuel/air mix, optimizing it according to the engine temperature and engine speed. It can control braking by releasing and reapplying the brakes whenever it detects the beginning of a skid. And it can record and display trip statistics, such as average speed and estimated time of arrival.

CHAPTER ELEVEN

THE PERSONAL COMPUTER

Personal computers have invaded the home and workplace. They were first marketed as kits for the tiny number of home enthusiasts who would enjoy the challenge of building number-crunching machines. Then ready-assembled home computers were sold as users realized that these new "microcomputers" could help them in their work and leisure.

The progress of computing since about 1945 has been driven by the development of ever better software (programs) and ever better hardware (machines).

Programs were developed that could be run without the user needing any programming skill by making choices from menus. The most significant step in making the computer "user-friendly" was the invention of the GUI (graphical user interface). The user moves a

A home computer can provide games, word-processing, education, email, Internet access, and more.

COMPUTER SYSTEMS

A desktop computer (top left) is controlled through a keyboard and a mouse. The documents it produces are stored on its built-in hard disk drive. Documents, with both words and pictures, can be printed out by a printer. A scanner can translate pictures into electronic data that can be entered into the computer. A laptop computer can rival the performance of the desktop computer. A tablet can have amazing power for its size, which is enhanced if it can exchange data and programs with a desktop machine.

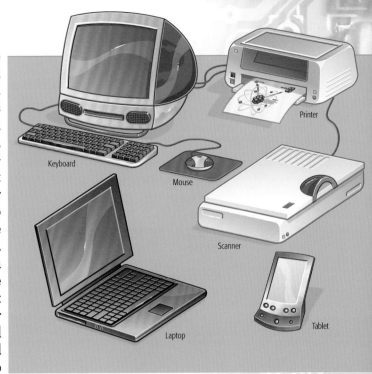

Printer

Keyboard

Mouse

Scanner

Laptop

Tablet

pointer called a cursor over the screen with a hand-operated device called a mouse and "clicks on" an icon (picture) representing the desired action.

At the same time, electronics technology progressed. The machines became faster, and their memory capacity grew bigger. In 1977 two of the earliest home computers, the Commodore PET and the Apple II, each had 4 kilobytes of RAM and 14 kilobytes of ROM. Many personal computers used audiocassette tapes to load and save programs and data. Processor speeds at this time were typically less than 5 MHz (1 MHz = 1 megahertz, or 1 million cycles per second). This is the number of basic steps

that the computer performs each second (many steps are needed to carry out even the simplest task, such as adding 2 and 2).

A typical modern home computer can have 8 GB or more of RAM and comparable amounts of ROM—and also possesses a huge amount of extra computing power dedicated to driving sophisticated sound systems and color video displays. Hard drives now hold 500 gigabytes or more. And processor speeds have moved into the gigahertz (1 billion cycles per second) range. Large and sophisticated programs are loaded from CD-ROMs or downloaded (that is, received) from the Internet.

COMPUTER NETWORKS

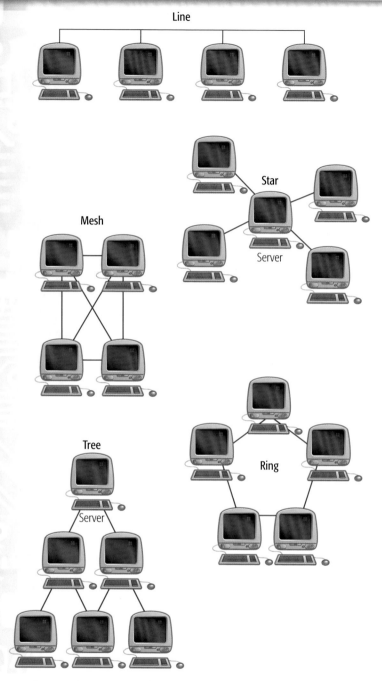

Computer networks can be organized in various ways, each with advantages and disadvantages. In the star arrangement, for example, if any computer other than the central one fails, it does not affect the others. However, if the central computer, or server, fails, links between all the others are affected. In some other networks all computers are equals.

PERIPHERAL DEVICES

The usefulness of the PC has been continually extended by a host of improvements in the electronics of peripherals, the devices that are hooked up to the computer. The mouse is a simple but crucial device. The side-to-side and backward-and-forward movement of a ball in its base is sensed by rollers or by light beams and turned into a stream of pulses that is sent to the computer, where it is turned into vertical and horizontal movements of the cursor. Buttons and sometimes a wheel are built into the mouse to send further commands.

Other input devices include keyboards and scanners. The keyboard resembles and works like a typewriter keyboard on which data is typed in. Scanners convert a picture or a page of text into "machine-readable" form. The image is stored as a sequence of digits in the computer's memory. Portable, handheld scanners have been developed, so that information can be read in, at a library for example, stored, and transferred to a computer later.

Another common output device is a printer. There have been many types of printer, but the laser printer now predominates in offices and many homes. It works like a photocopier. A laser beam sweeps over a rotating, electrically charged metal cylinder. The light causes charge to be lost in some places, so that a pattern of

Complicated systems are designed with the aid of computer programs called CAD (computer-aided design) software. Individual items can be rapidly and easily reshaped or repositioned, and the whole scene can be viewed from any direction and at various magnifications.

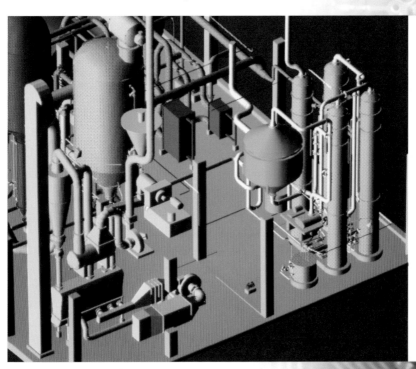

Today, most office employees have one or more computers at their desks. They can also use remote access programs to connect to their office computers while they are away from their desks.

electric charges is formed on the drum that is a copy of the image. Toner (ink powder) is attracted to the drum at the places where the charge is strongest and is pressed onto a sheet of paper. The toner is pressed against the paper by a heated roller, bonding it tightly to the paper. The laser printer is quiet and fast. A cheaper alternative, especially for color printing, is the inkjet printer. This type of printer fires jets of ink droplets at the paper to form the image.

COMPUTERS AT WORK

Previously a large company might have had a single, expensive mainframe computer to serve all its needs. Some individual employees had terminals on their desks, enabling them to use the main computer. With the arrival of the microchip more and more employees acquired personal computers instead. Electronic mail, known as e-mail, was developed to help them communicate with one another.

The PC revolutionized many industries. Printing companies had been computerized long before the microchip; now computerization spread back along the production process to the editors and designers in publishing companies, who could now edit and design every detail of a book, newspaper, or magazine at their desk.

An engineer could design a product using computer-aided design

(CAD) software. A design could rapidly go through hundreds of stages, being improved at every step, with the computer providing a "photorealistic" image of the final product, if needed. At the end the information that was in the design was turned into the specifications for each component of the product, which machine tools would automatically produce.

COMPUTERS ON THE GO

As PCs became more indispensable in business, executives increasingly wanted to take them along when they worked outside the office. Portable computers evolved from cumbersome suitcase-sized machines to slim, light laptops. A major development was the flat screen. It uses an LCD, or liquid-crystal display. The image is formed as a pattern of small voltages is applied across the screen. This causes liquid in the display to become clearer or darker, depending on the voltage. The screen is backlit, and the light is blocked to varying degrees, forming the optical image.

Many laptop computers now have built-in CD-ROM drives, as well as hard disc drives with several gigabytes of storage. They can be linked to mobile phones, meaning that the user can maintain e-mail communication with his or her office and is able to surf the Internet while on the move.

Tablets are now formidable, too. Some are designed as powerful stand-alone computers. Others are designed to exchange data readily with a PC when dropped into a desktop cradle or over a wireless Internet connection. Data can be entered, and many basic computing functions can be carried out while the user is away from the PC; more advanced work is done on the PC and transferred as necessary.

Lightweight, portable laptops make it easy to work from libraries, coffee shops, and even outside!

CHAPTER TWELVE

ELECTRONICS TODAY AND TOMORROW

Sometimes it is easy to overlook a revolutionary change, such as the change brought about by electronics, because it is so widespread and it affects everything. We rarely think about the host of things made possible by electronics that were not possible for our grandparents, from remote-controlled TVs to airliners that fly themselves.

We take it for granted that we can make a photocopy of any document quickly and easily on the copier in an office or library, or at a school, or in a copying store. Yet making such copies was quite a complicated photographic process 50 years ago. Alternatively, if copies of a document were going to be needed, special "carbon paper" would be used that made one or two extra copies of the document as it was typed.

Millions of dollars' worth of stocks are traded through the Tokyo Stock Exchange via global electronic links every day. Market information is displayed electronically on giant wall displays.

Computers occupied whole rooms and rarely had keyboards or display screens. Programs were in the form of packs of punched cards, and the only output was in the form of an often bulky printout.

SPECIAL EFFECTS

The special effects that were used in movies before the 1960s are amusing to us today. We are accustomed to impressively realistic and spectacular effects, created by hundreds of hours of processing of images by some of the most advanced supercomputers in the world. In TV programs and commercials we see images recolored, reshaped, mixed, played forward and backward in slow motion or fast motion, and perfectly synchronized with words and music, where once almost the only editing technique available was to cut film into pieces and splice them together. Once nearly all TV programs were broadcast live; now most of them are prerecorded on videotape.

An unseen consequence of instant communications is the effect on our standard of living of international trading. Billions of dollars' worth of goods, services, and stocks are traded around the world every day. A financial crisis in Asia can affect the markets of the rest of the world within hours, and bring stock values falling and send commodity prices rising within hours. Some financial panics have been blamed on the automated buying and selling of stocks by computerized trading systems, moving huge amounts of money before human beings can notice anything wrong and intervene.

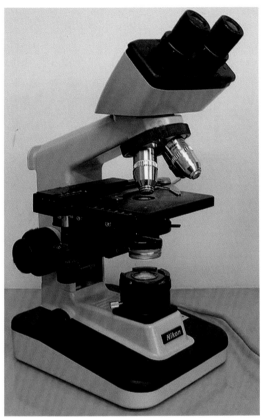

In an optical microscope, a laser beam scans the specimen, and a computer processes the reflected light to produce a colored image.

We take it for granted that we can see events from around the world on TV as they happen, with high-quality color and sound. But the first crude, blurred intercontinental TV images were transmitted only in 1962 via Telstar, the first true communications satellite to be launched into orbit.

Forty years ago clocks and watches were all mechanical. They had to be wound and corrected regularly—often daily. A calculator was a bulky desktop machine that could do little more than add, subtract, multiply, and divide.

Sunlight is converted into electricity by suitable semiconductor materials. The solar panels on this roof generate enough electrical energy to power the electrical devices in the home.

But the effects of rapid trading are most of the time more benign: A steady, unnoticed contribution to the world's rising standard of living.

CELL PHONES

The electronics revolution has touched everyone except those in the most remote areas of the world's poorest countries. Ordinary people in the richer countries can stay connected with each other all the time. The cell phone, or mobile phone, has put everyone permanently in touch with one another.

Cell phones are UHF (ultrahigh frequency) transmitters and receivers. In a given area, called a cell, they communicate with an automatic base station. The phones are low power, so they do not interfere with other users in distant cells. The phones in neighboring cells use different frequencies. When users switch on their phones, a "conversation" called registration takes place with the nearest base station to identify the phone and make sure its location is known to the cell phone network. Immensely complex computing is needed to automatically switch a phone's frequency to a new one if the user moves from one cell to another and also to route calls from one cell to the next.

News correspondents who are on assignments away from their offices now regularly write their stories on laptops and send them by e-mail via cell phones. In parts of the world where there is as yet poor coverage from a cell phone network, they use satellite phones, which beam their messages directly from a radio dish to a communications satellite far out in a 24-hour orbit. Soon it will be possible for mobile phones to work anywhere in the world without the need for the special radio dish. They will be linked via swarms of satellites in low orbits.

The cell phone is rapidly developing into a fully fledged communication device. It can offer not only voice communication but also the ability to send and receive e-mails and to browse the Internet, with a color display built in. With the new satellite systems it will be possible to operate as effectively in the most remote desert as in a city.

GLOBAL POSITIONING SYSTEM

Another system of 24 satellites, which comprise the Global Positioning System (GPS), provides accurate positional information. GPS units can be hand-held or mounted in a car or boat. Smart phones also use GPS. Each satellite orbits once in 24 hours and transmits its own characteristic identification signal as well as a series of continuous time signals.

The user's unit detects the very accurately timed signals from any four of the satellites that are above the horizon at any one time. One satellite provides a

A handheld unit tells this user his precise location thanks to the system of GPS (Global Positioning System) satellites. Precisely timed signals from several of the dozens of orbiting satellites are converted into his latitude and longitude. The direction and distance to his destination can also be computed and displayed.

In a warehouse, laser beams read the barcodes on packages and instantly convert them into information, such as the contents of the box and the price of the goods.

reference signal; the other three satellites provide bearing signals. The computer in the user's unit calculates the position from the tiny differences in the times taken for the signals to arrive from the different satellites. The position is displayed either as a grid reference or in terms of latitude and longitude. The standard service tells users their positions to an accuracy of 100 meters (330 feet). Even more precise positioning is possible with more complex equipment as used by, for example, the military, commercial airlines, and surveyors.

Despite the fact that electronic communications are now bringing the world into our homes, people still want to travel more and more. The car is already packed with electronic equipment to enhance its comfort, efficiency and safety (as described on page 53). But the electronically most advanced form of transport is the airplane.

Large passenger planes are now flying robots. Once the plane is in the air, the pilot and the copilot (there are only two flight crew on modern airliners) merely keep watch over the controls that are flying the plane. The crew is needed in emergencies, but in ordinary flight the autopilot monitors the plane's speed and direction, and compares them with the flight plan that has been programmed in before takeoff.

It operates the control surfaces on the wings and controls engine speed. Monitoring the navigational signals from radio beacons on the ground, it flies the airplane all the way to its destination. In bad conditions it can also land the plane automatically at well-equipped airports that have the necessary systems. The two pilots rest their hands on the joysticks, or control columns, while this happens, ready to take over in case something goes wrong.

If during flight a pilot takes over control and tries to make the plane perform some dangerous maneuver, such as diving too steeply or climbing at too great an angle, the autopilot first sounds a warning siren. If the pilot persists, the autopilot shakes the joystick vigorously. And if this produces no response, the autopilot takes over control and levels out the plane, and corrects the engine speed.

LOOKING TO THE FUTURE

Electronic systems may have some rivals soon. It is now possible to boost computing power by using light beams rather than electric currents to carry information. Experimental "optical chips" have already been made. Biological computers may also be developed, using the

Technology that was first developed for military radar now makes it possible to cook using microwaves.

DNA and RNA molecules that store and pass on genetic information in living cells. Such radically new kinds of computer could be very fast, but their input and output would continue to be by electronic signals.

There may also be obstacles to further progress in electronics. At the moment, more and more complex circuits are being etched onto microchips every year. But there may be a minimum size at which components can be made before electrons start to "leak" out of them. When this limit is reached, it may not be possible to go any further in the direction of miniaturization.

However, to compensate for this, it might prove possible to develop a new kind of computer called a quantum computer, using the mysterious ability of electrons to be in different states simultaneously. This could herald another leap in computing power.

However much electronics will be transformed in the next half-century, in ways we cannot possibly foresee, we can be certain that it will continue to be the bedrock of our scientific and industrial society.

Airliners depend on electronics to carry out every function, from navigation and radio communications to moving the control surfaces and lowering the undercarriage. This use of electronics in airplane construction is called "fly by wire."

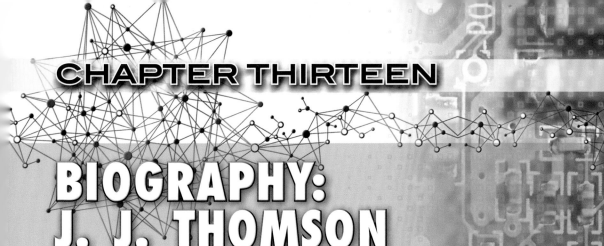

CHAPTER THIRTEEN

BIOGRAPHY:
J. J. THOMSON

Joseph John "J. J." Thomson's father wanted him to grow up to be an engineer. However, that did not work out. Instead, Thomson became a physicist and went on to discover the electron. Prior to Thomson's discovery, it was thought that the atom was the smallest particle.

Thomson was born in Cheetham Hill, England, a suburb of Manchester, on December 18, 1856. His father, named Joseph James Thomson, was a third generation bookseller. His mother was named Emma Swindells, and he had a younger brother named Frederick Vernon Thomson. Thomson's father had him apply for an engineering apprenticeship at Sharp-Stewart and Company, which was a very reputable maker of locomotives.

J. J. Thomson's discoveries led to great advances in the field of physics.

KEY DATES

1856 December 18, born in
      Cheetham Hill, England

1870 Begins studies at
      Owens College

1880 Graduates from Trinity College

1884 Appointed Cavendish Professor
      of Experimental Physics

1892 Marries Rose Paget

1897 Travels to the United States

1897 Discovers the electron

1906 Wins the Nobel Prize in Physics

1918 Becomes Master of Trinity College

1940 August 30, dies and is buried at
      Westminster Abbey

However, the apprenticeship program was so popular that there was a two year waiting list. Thomson's father, on the advice of a friend, enrolled him at Owens College while keeping him on the waiting list for the apprenticeship. Young J. J. was accepted and began college at just 14 years old. Thomson regarded this "accident" as "the most critical event in [his] life which determined [his] career."

OWENS COLLEGE AND A GROWING INTEREST IN PHYSICS

Starting college at 14 was not a common thing at the time. It was about as uncommon then as it would be today. In fact, after Thomson was accepted, Owens College raised the minimum age of admission to 16 years old in order to prevent the enrollment of anyone else so young. It was in his second year at Owens College that Thomson was introduced to physics. Thomson was immediately fascinated.

When Thomson was 16 years old, his father died. With his father's death, Thomson was no longer able to pursue his career in engineering, because the apprenticeship required a payment that his mother could not afford. So, instead of quitting college and becoming an engineer, Thomson continued on at Owens. With scholarships and his mother's hard work, Thomson was able to afford to stay on at college.

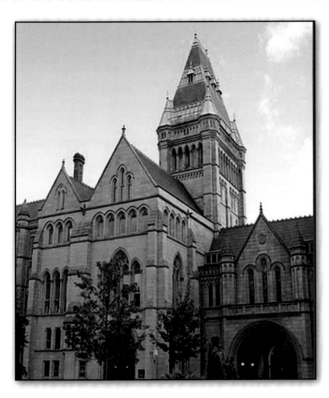

Owens College later merged with other universities and today its buildings are part of the University of Manchester.

Thomson was encouraged by his mathematics professor to finish two more years at Owens, studying physics and mathematics, and then to apply for a scholarship to Trinity College, which was a part of the University of Cambridge. He failed to get the scholarship on his first attempt, but tried again the next year and got it.

TRINITY COLLEGE AND CAVENDISH LABORATORY

Thomson completed his undergraduate studies in 1880, with a degree in mathematics. He finished Second Wrangler. This was a distinction given to the student who finished second in his class. Finishing first in the class was very competitive and Thomson was beaten by Joseph Larmor, who became a prominent mathematical physicist.

After graduation, Thomson began working at the Cavendish Laboratory, at the University of Cambridge, under Lord Rayleigh. The Cavendish Laboratory was founded in 1874. James Clerk Maxwell, developer of the basic equations of electromagnetism, was the first Cavendish professor. Lord Rayleigh, who discovered the element argon, a discovery that earned him a Nobel Prize in 1904, was the second professor. It was with these two accomplished scientists that Thomson learned to conduct experiments. With his focus up to that point mostly on mathematics, he did not have much lab experience. However, he quickly caught up and excelled. Cavendish Laboratory went on to produce seven Nobel Prize winners and twenty-seven Fellows of the Royal Society.

Lord Rayleigh resigned in 1884. Thomson decided to apply for his position, as professor. At this time, Thomson was still in his twenties and many people did not think he would get the job because of his age. However, in 1884 he was named Cavendish Professor of Experimental Physics. In the same year, he was also named a Fellow by the Royal Society of London. Not everyone at Cambridge approved of Thomson's appointment as professor. Many other professors thought him too young and inexperienced. Again, Thomson proved them wrong.

GEORGE JOHNSTONE STONEY

George Johnstone Stoney was born in Ireland in 1826. He studied mathematics and physics at Trinity College, in Dublin, and received his master's degree in 1852. Stoney is best remembered for introducing the term "electron" in 1891 to describe a basic unit of electric charge. Just a few years later, the word electron began to be used to describe Thomson's corpuscles.

Thomson was already very accomplished for someone so young, but he continued to achieve more and more. In 1892, he published his treatise, *Notes of Recent Researches in Electricity and Magnetism*. He focused much of his early work on electrical conduction in gases. Thomson traveled to the United States in 1896 where he gave a series of lectures at Princeton University. The lectures were about his research work at the time. In 1897, he published *Discharge of Electricity through Gases*, which was based on the series of lectures.

MAJOR DISCOVERY

Thomson's most important discovery, the electron, was made in 1897. Thomson had been focusing his research on cathode rays. Cathode rays are produced inside of a cathode ray tube, which is a glass, vacuum-like tube. There are two plates within the tube, one of which is negatively charged. When the plates are attached to a high-voltage source, the negatively charged plate produces an invisible ray. When the ray beams down the tube and hits the end, it emits a bright

The first commercially-made television sets were sold in the 1930s and used cathode ray tubes, such as the one seen here.

light. Cathode rays were not very well understood in the late 1800s and were a popular topic of study among physicists. Physicists were trying to understand what the ray was made up of.

Many physicists at the time believed that the cathode rays were similar to light. But a few physicists like Heinrich Hertz and Thomson believed the rays were made up of particles. Hertz conducted an experiment in which he observed the cathode ray passing through a thin sheet of gold. To Hertz, it seemed impossible that a particle could pass through a solid.

Thomson set out to build on Hertz's experiments. He realized that the cathode ray would move away from negatively charged plates and that it would move towards positively charged plates. This meant that the ray was negatively charged.

Thomson was able to balance the cathode ray using electric fields and magnetic fields. With the knowledge of how to balance the field Thomson was able to calculate the velocity of the ray. With the velocity, Thomson was then able to calculate the deflection on the ray in the electric field alone. With that information, Thomson was finally able to calculate the charge of the particles in the ray. What he had found was a particle with a charge two thousand times greater than a hydrogen ion. Hydrogen was the lightest particle known at the time of Thomson's experiment, in 1897. Thomson was able to confirm that the particles that make up the cathode ray were two thousand times lighter than hydrogen, and this was why they were able to pass through solid objects.

Thomson initially used aluminum to create the cathode rays, but he went on to experiment with different metals. His experiments with other metals produced the same results. The charge of the particles remained the same no matter what type of metal he used to produce the rays. Thomson concluded that the rays were made up of particles even smaller than atoms. He named these particles corpuscles. Thomson concluded that corpuscles were a universal part of matter, meaning that they form part of all atoms in the universe.

Thomson announced his discovery on April 30, 1897, in a lecture to the Royal Institution. He presented three hypotheses based on his experiments. The first was that cathode rays are charged particles. The second, that corpuscles are

J. J. Thomson is seen here (front row center) with his research students at the Cavendish Laboratory at Cambridge. To his left is Paul Langevin, who would later work with Pierre Curie and become a prominent French physicist.

J. J. Thomson is seen here at work at the Cavendish Laboratory.

elements of the atom. And the third, that corpuscles are the only constituent of the atom. Initially, fellow scientists were skeptical. However, they were convinced by Thomson's thorough experiments. Of course, his third hypotheses turned out to be false. Scientists immediately started calling Thomson's corpuscles electrons. Electron was a term coined by another scientist named George Johnstone Stoney to describe something else. But, with the discovery of corpuscles, the term

was taken to describe them. Thomson did not approve of the name "electron" and did not come around to it until twenty years later.

Now that scientists knew that the atom was made up of smaller particles, the question became: How do the particles form an atom? Thomson had his own theory about this. His theory is often called the "plum pudding" model. Thomson believed that the negatively charged electrons swarmed

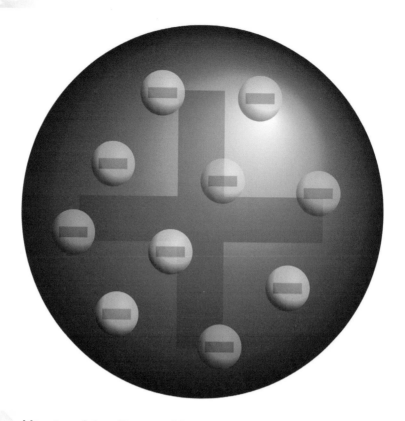

The "plum pudding" model is illustrated here as a large form of positive charge (+) with particles of negative charge (-) scattered throughout.

together in a cloud of massless positive charge. This theory was proved incorrect by Thomson's own student, Ernest Rutherford. Rutherford proposed the idea of a nucleus. He believed that the atom resembled a tiny universe, with a positively charged nucleus at its center and electrons floating around it. Rutherford's idea of the nucleus was revolutionary, but his structure of the atom was quite oversimplified. It was later discovered that the nucleus was made up of even smaller particles, called protons and neutrons.

OTHER DISCOVERIES AND ACCOMPLISHMENTS

Discovering the electron may seem like quite a life accomplishment, but Thomson did not stop there. He continued his research and continued to make groundbreaking discoveries. In 1907, Thomson and his student Francis Aston began researching positive rays. They were hoping to discover the particle that carried a positive charge. Thomson found that each element had a different positive ion and that the element neon had two positive ions. These ions are known as isotopes.

Isotopes had previously been identified in radioactive elements, but Thomson was the first to identify them in a nonradioactive element. This discovery was not as well accepted as the electron, and many scientists doubted Thomson. Aston continued his research, though he stopped for several years due to World War I. After the war, Aston continued his research. In 1919, he invented the mass spectrograph. Mass spectrometers

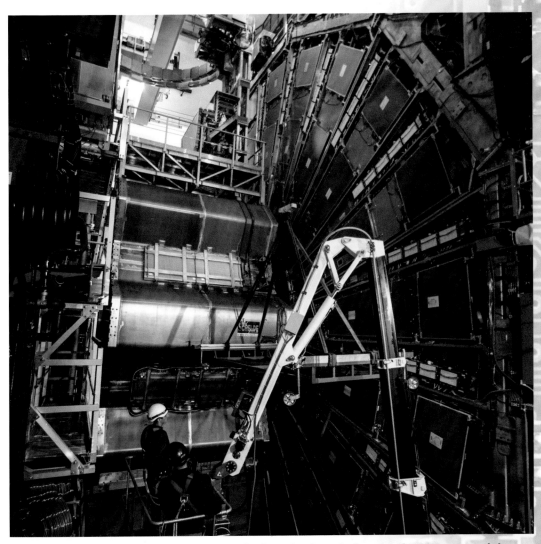

The discoveries of Thomson, Rutherford, and others led to the development of the field of nuclear physics and modern equipment such as particle accelerators.

separate ions by mass. They do this by accelerating the ions through a magnetic field. Charged particles will curve as they go through the magnetic field. The larger the charged particle, the less its path will bend. Using his invention, Aston identified 212 natural isotopes. He won the Nobel Prize in Chemistry for his discovery of the mass spectrograph and the discovery of nonradioactive isotopes. Though Thomson was not directly responsible for the invention of the mass spectrograph it was his curiosity and encouragement that led his student Aston to the discovery.

Thomson's interest in the composition of atoms never dwindled. In 1904, he again traveled to the United States. This time he gave a series of lectures at Yale University. The lectures were about his suggestions as to the structure of the atom. He spoke about separating

The original Cavendish Laboratory, seen here, was founded in 1874. In the early 1970s the laboratory was moved to a new site in West Cambridge.

The first mass spectrograph was designed by Francis Aston. Aston also devised the Whole Number Rule, which states that, the mass of the oxygen isotope being defined, all other isotopes have masses that are very nearly whole numbers.

different kinds of atoms using positive rays. Thomson published many works on his research including *The Structure of Light* (1907), *The Corpuscular Theory of Matter* (1907), *Rays of Positive Electricity* (1913), and *The Electron in Chemistry* (1923).

In 1906, Thomson was awarded the Nobel Prize in Physics. He received the prize "in recognition of the great merits of his theoretical and experimental investigations on the conduction of electricity by gases." Thomson was the recipient of numerous other honors, such as the Hodgkins Medal (from the Smithsonian Institute) and the Copley Medal. Though Thomson studied at Owens and Trinity, he held many honorary degrees. He received honorary degrees from Columbia, Princeton, Oxford, and the Sorbonne among many others.

In 1918, Thomson became Master of Trinity College. He remained in that position for the remainder of his life.

Thomson spent the last 22 years of his life as master of Trinity College, part of the University of Cambridge.

PERSONAL LIFE

Thomson married Rose Paget in 1892. Rose had been one of Thomson's students at Cambridge. She was one of the first women permitted into advanced university studies. They had two children, Joan and George. George Paget Thomson followed in his father's footsteps and became a physicist. He attended Trinity College and eventually worked as a researcher under his father. George's work as a physicist was interrupted by World War I. He survived the war and went on to win a Nobel Prize in 1937. He was awarded the Nobel Prize for his work with electrons. He discovered that they behave as waves despite being particles.

J. J. Thomson was well-liked and unpretentious, despite being a Nobel Prize winner. Besides physics, Thomson's other hobby was gardening.

He published an autobiography in 1936 called *Recollections and Reflections*. Thomson died on August 30, 1940. His ashes are buried at Westminster Abbey near other great scientists, including Sir Isaac Newton and Charles Darwin.

During World War II, George Paget Thomson, seen here with his father, worked on the military applications of nuclear physics, including the possibility of building an atomic bomb.

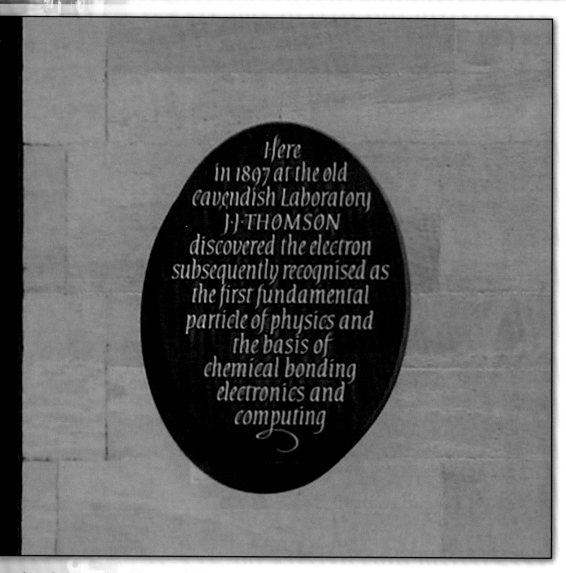

This plaque at the old Cavendish Laboratory commemorates the important and influential work of J. J. Thomson.

SCIENTIFIC BACKGROUND

1869 German physicist
Johann Hittorf
is the first to
observe cathode rays

1891 Henrich Hertz discovers
that cathode rays can
penetrate solid objects

1891 George Johnstone Stoney
coins the word "electron"

1908 Ernest Rutherford receives
the Nobel Prize in Chemistry

1911 Ernest Rutherford discovers
the nucleus

1919 Francis Aston invents the
mass spectrograph

1922 Francis Aston wins the
Nobel Prize in Chemistry

1928 Alexander Fleming
discovers penicillin

1930 Pluto is discovered and for
over 70 years is considered
the ninth planet of the solar system

1932 John Cockcroft and Earnest
Walton split a lithium atom

1932 James Chadwick discovers the
neutron using scattering data

POLITICAL AND CULTURAL BACKGROUND

1856 The Crimean War, a conflict between Russia and the allies of France, Britain, the Ottoman Empire, and Sardinia ends

1861 The US Civil War begins between the Union forces of the North and the Confederate forces of the South

1865 Abraham Lincoln, president of the United States, is assassinated in Washington, D.C.

1870 The Franco-Prussian War begins

1883 Krakatoa, a volcano in Indonesia, erupts killing over 30,000 people

1883 The Brooklyn Bridge, the longest suspension bridge in the world at the time, opens, connecting the borough of Brooklyn with the island of Manhattan

1890 Yosemite becomes a US National Park

1896 The first modern Olympics are held in Athens, Greece

1900 Kodak introduces the Brownie camera

1901 Queen Victoria, the monarch of the United Kingdom of Great Britain and Ireland, dies at the age of 81

1903 Produced by Thomas Edison, *The Great Train Robbery*, the first narrative silent film, is released

1917 The United States enters World War I

1918 The Spanish flu epidemic spreads around the world, killing between 50 and 100 million people

1929 The stock market crashes, signaling the beginning of the Great Depression

1937 Pilot Amelia Earhart disappears during an attempt to fly around the world

alternating current (AC) Electric current that flows first in one direction, then in the other, alternating many times each second. AC is used for domestic electricity supply and many other electrical applications.

amplifier A device that increases the voltage or current (usually alternating current) of a signal.

anode A positive electrical terminal on a device such as a battery. Electrons flow into the device through the anode. See also *cathode*.

atom The smallest part of a chemical element that can exist on its own. It has a central nucleus, surrounded by electrons.

base The middle part of a junction transistor. A small signal voltage applied to the base causes a large change in the output voltage or current.

battery A device that generates electric current by a chemical reaction.

bit A unit of information representing a choice between two possibilities. In the binary system of notation, in which all numbers are written with the numerals 0 and 1 only, a single 0 or 1 represents one bit. See also *byte*.

byte (B) A sequence of bits, usually 8. In computing, this means a sequence of 8 digits—that is, 0's or 1's.

capacitance Also called capacity, the ratio of the stored electric charge on an electrical device or other object to the voltage applied to it.

capacitor Also called a condenser, a device that stores electric charge.

cathode A negative electrical terminal on a device such as a battery. Electrons flow into or out of the device through the cathode. See also *anode*.

cathode ray A stream of electrons produced by the heated cathode in a vacuum tube.

CD Abbreviation for compact disc, a device on which data can be recorded. It is a plastic platter on whose surface are tiny pits representing the data. The pits are "read" with a laser beam. A CD can store sound, pictures, movies, or computer data.

CD-ROM A CD on which computer data or programs are stored.

channel In a field-effect transistor the part of the device through which the main current flows. See also *gate*.

charge A property of some subatomic particles and some larger objects that makes them exert forces on one another. Charge can be of two kinds, positive or negative.

circuit A network of electrical components that performs some function.

collector The part of a transistor toward which the charge carriers (electrons or holes) flow.

compact disc See *CD*.

conductor A material or object that allows electric current (or heat) to flow through it. See also *insulator*.

Crookes tube An early experimental vacuum tube in which cathode rays were generated.

current A flow of electric charge. The current from the domestic electricity supply, from generators, and from batteries consists of a flow of electrons. Positively charged ions form part of the current inside some types of battery, moving in the opposite direction from a flow of electrons.

DC See *direct current*.

diode An electronic device, having two electrodes, that allows current to pass through in one direction only. Early diodes were vacuum tubes; modern ones use solid-state electronics.

direct current (DC) Electric current that flows in one direction all the time, though it may vary in strength.

disk An electronic recording device. A magnetic disk is coated with a material that can easily be magnetized in one direction or another at each poicnt by applying a magnetic field, making the surface of the disk resemble a vast collection of tiny magnets. The direction of the disk's magnetic field at each point represents one bit of information. See also *CD*; *CD-ROM*.

drain The end of a field-effect transistor from which charge carriers flow into the external circuit. See also *gate; source*.

DRAM Dynamic RAM (random- access memory) that loses information stored in it when the current to it is switched off. See also *SRAM*.

DVD Abbreviation for digital versatile disk, a type of optical disk that can store much more information, and retrieve it at a higher speed, than an ordinary CD.

electron A subatomic particle, found in every atom, that carries negative charge. Most currents consist of electrons in motion.

electron shell A grouping of electrons in an atom. Electrons in a given shell have approximately the same energy. Each shell can hold only a certain number of electrons.

emitter The part of a transistor from which the charge carriers (electrons or holes) flow.

energy The ability of a system to bring about changes in other systems. In electricity the stored chemical energy of a battery can make electric current flow. An electrical generator uses the energy of fuel to make electric current flow. Electric current is converted into other forms of energy where required (e.g., light in a lightbulb).

EPROM Erasable–programmable ROM (read-only memory). The contents of this type of ROM can be deleted as a whole, often by being illuminated with ultraviolet light, before being rewritten.

farad (F) The SI unit of capacitance. If 1 coulomb of charge stored on an object increases its voltage by 1 volt, it has a capacitance of 1 farad. The farad is a very large unit, so the microfarad (1 uF, 1 millionth of a farad) or the picofarad (1 pF, 1 billionth of a farad) are more usually used.

floppy disk A small, flexible magnetic disk used to store relatively small quantities of computer data. The standard type is 3.5 in. (8.9 cm) across and holds 1.44 megabytes of data.

force An influence that changes the shape, position, or movement of an object.

frequency The rate at which some cyclic process repeats. The frequency of alternating current is the number of times per second that the current reaches a maximum in one direction.

gate Part of a field-effect transistor to which a signal voltage is applied. It causes a large variation in the flow of current through the transistor. See also *drain; source*.

gigabyte (GB) In common usage 1,000 megabytes.

hard disk A rigid magnetic disk used to store large quantities of computer data.

hole A position in the crystal lattice of a semiconductor material where an electron is lacking. When a neighboring electron jumps into the gap, the hole effectively moves in the opposite direction.

insulator A material or object that is a poor conductor of electric current (or heat).

integrated circuit A solid-state electronics circuit made from a single piece of semiconductor material.

ion An atom or molecule that has lost or gained one or more electrons so that it has an electrical charge.

kilobyte (kB) 1,024 (2^{10}) bytes.

klystron A vacuum tube designed to generate high-power microwaves.

LCD Abbreviation for liquid-crystal display, used in calculators and watches. Characters appear dark against a backlit or reflective background.

LED Abbreviation for light-emitting diode, a solid-state diode that gives out light when electric current passes through it.

megabyte 1,048,576 (2^{20}) bytes.

microchip A piece of semiconductor material in which an integrated circuit has been made; it is literally chipped from a wafer in which hundreds of identical circuits are made.

***n*-type semiconductor** A semiconductor material in which current consists mostly of electrons in motion.

ohm (Ω) The SI unit of resistance.

oscillator An electronic circuit that generates an alternating current or alternating voltage.

oscilloscope An electronic device that displays a

signal as a graph on the screen of a cathode-ray tube.

PCB Abbreviation for printed-circuit board, a rigid board acting as the support for a printed circuit.

photoelectric effect The ejection of electrons from certain solids, especially metals, when light falls on them. The effect is used in many devices, often to signal when a light beam has been broken, as in a burglar alarm or elevator door control.

power The rate of expending energy.

printed circuit An electronic circuit consisting of components attached to a board or to flexible plastic and connected by lines of metal printed onto the support. See also *PCB*.

p-**type semiconductor** A semiconductor material in which current consists mostly of moving holes.

quantum The smallest amount by which energy or some other physical quantity can change. An electron gives out or takes in a quantum of energy when it jumps between electron shells in an atom.

RAM Abbreviation for random-access memory, memory storage in a computer in which any item of information can be retrieved for processing equally quickly.

random-access memory See *RAM*.

read-only memory See *ROM*.

rectifier An electronic device through which current can flow in one direction only. It converts alternating current to direct current.

resistance A measure of how a material or a component resists the passage of electric current through it. The higher the resistance, the less current will pass when a given voltage is applied.

resistor An electrical component with a known resistance, used to regulate current and voltage in a circuit.

ROM Abbreviation for read-only memory: in a computer, memory whose contents are not altered in operation.

semiconductor A material that has a resistance intermediate between those of an insulator and a conductor. See also n-*type semiconductor;* p-*type semiconductor.*

shell See *electron shell.*

solid-state electronics The science and technology of using semiconductor materials rather than vacuum tubes to make electronic devices.

source The end of a field-effect transistor at which charge carriers flow in from the external circuit. See also *drain; gate.*

SRAM Static RAM (random-access memory). This type of RAM does not lose its stored information if the current through it is interrupted. See also *DRAM.*

transistor A solid-state electronics device that amplifies a small signal current or voltage and turns it into a large output current or voltage. The two major types are called junction transistors and field-effect transistors.

triode An electronic device that has three electrodes. The word usually refers to vacuum tube triodes, which formerly were widely used as amplifiers.

vacuum tube An electronic device consisting of a glass vessel containing a partial vacuum through which electrons flow from a heated cathode.

valve An old name for a vacuum tube, so called because current flows only one way through a vacuum tube, just as a fluid flows only one way through a mechanical valve.

volt The SI unit of voltage.

voltage The difference in electric potential between two points. It is measured in volts.

wafer A slice cut from a cylinder of semiconductor material in which hundreds of integrated circuits have been made. The wafer is cut up into microchips.

watt (W) The SI unit of power, equal to a rate of expending energy of 1 joule per second.

X-ray Penetrating electromagnetic radiation of very short wavelength and high energy. X-rays are produced by electrons jumping between the deepest, innermost electron shells of the atom.

Computer History Museum
1401 N. Shoreline Boulevard
Mountain View, CA 94043
605-810-1010
Web site: http://www.computerhistory.
org/
This museum, located in Silicon Valley,
follows the history of computers,
from early models the size of entire
rooms to today's smart phones that
fit in the palm of a person's hand.
Special exhibits showcase the histo-
ries of semiconductors and
microprocessors, and the growing
collection includes early personal
computers, robots, and early arcade
video games.

Electric Auto Association
323 Los Altos Drive
Aptos, CA 95003
831-688-8669
Web site: http://www.electricauto.org/
This organization, formed in 1967, seeks
to promote the advancement and
widespread use of electric vehicles.
The group shares information about
new developments in technology,
encourages experimentation in the
construction of new electric models,
and organizes exhibits and events to
inform the general public about the
benefits of electric vehicles.

Museum of the Moving Image
36-01 35th Avenue
Astoria, NY 11106
718-784-0077
Website: http://www.movingimage.us/

The Museum of the Moving Image cele-
brates the history, artistic vision, and
technology of film, television, and
digital media. The core exhibition features over 1,400 artifacts related the
moving images, from 19th century
optical toys to today's video games.

National Atomic Testing Museum
755 E. Flamingo Rd.
Las Vegas, NV 89119
702-794-5151
Web site: http://www.nationalatomictest-
ingmuseum.org/
This museum, part of the Smithsonian
Institute, traces the conception,
development, and testing of the
atomic bomb. Exhibits on such top-
ics as radiation and underground
testing are on permanent display.

Nobel Prize
Sturegatan 14
Box 5232
SE-102 45 Stockholm
Sweden
+46 8 663 27 69
Web site: www.nobelprize.org
The Nobel Prize is awarded each year in
the six categories of Physics,
Chemistry, Economic Science,
Literature, Physiology or Medicine,
and Peace. It is considered one of the
most prestigious awards in the
world. Winners receive a gold medal,
a diploma, and a monetary prize of
over $1 million.

Paley Center for Media
25 West 52nd Street
New York, NY 10019
212-621-6600
Web site: http://www.paleycenter.org/
Formerly the Museum of Television and
 Radio, the Paley Center for Media
 traces the history of television and
 radio and their place in culture
 and society.

Smithsonian National Air and Space
 Museum
Independence Avenue at 6th Street SW
Washington, DC 20560
202-633-2214
Web site: http://airandspace.si.edu/visit/
 mall/
This museum showcases the history of
 air and space exploration and fea-
 tures the Apollo 11 Command
 Module, the Albert Einstein
 Planetarium, an observatory open to
 the public, and much more.

World Nuclear Association
22a St. James's Square
London SW1Y 4JH
United Kingdom
+44 (0)20 7451 1520
Web site: http://www.world-nuclear.org/
This organization, based in the United
 Kingdom, represents people and
 organizations involved in nuclear
 power around the world. Their Web
 site includes basic information on
 nuclear power as well as charts, out-
 lines, and scientific papers with
 up-to-date information about
 nuclear power.

WEB SITES

Due to the changing nature of Internet
links, Rosen Publishing has developed
an online list of Web sites related to the
subject of this book. This site is updated
regularly. Please use this link to access
the list:

http://www.rosenlinks.com/CORE/Elec

Abramson, Albert. *The History of Television, 1880 to 1941*. Jefferson, NC: McFarland Publishing, 2009.

Bureau of Naval Personnel. *Basic Electricity*. Dover Books on Electrical Engineering. Mineola, NY: Dover Publications, 2012.

Fetter-Vorm, Jonathan. *Trinity: A Graphic History of the First Atomic Bomb*. New York: Hill & Wang, 2013.

Fox, Michael H. *Why We Need Nuclear Power: The Environmental Case*. Oxford, UK: Oxford University Press, 2014.

Gray, Theodore. *The Elements: A Visual Exploration of Every Known Atom in the Universe*. New York: Black Dog and Leventhal Publishers, 2012.

Herman, Stephen L. *Alternating Current Fundamentals*. Independence, KY: Delmar Learning, 2013.

Herman, Stephen L. *Direct Current Fundamentals*. Independence, KY: Delmar Learning, 2013.

Kim, Dong-Won. *Leadership and Creativity: A History of the Cavendish Laboratory, 1871–1919*. New York: Springer Publishing Company, 2014.

Laramie, James, and John Lowry. *Electric Vehicles Technology Explained*. Hoboken, NJ: Wiley, 2013.

Lécuyer, Christopher. *Makers of the Microchip: A Documentary History of the Fairchild Semiconductor*. Cambridge, MA: MIT Press, 2011.

Navarro, Jaume. *A History of the Electron: J. J. Thomson and G. P. Thomson*. Cambridge, UK: Cambridge University Press, 2013.

Platt, Charles. *Encyclopedia of Electronic Components Volume 1: Resistors, Capacitors, Inductors, Switches, Encoders, Relays, Transistors*. Sebastopol, CA: Maker Media Inc., 2013.

Platt, Charles. *Encyclopedia of Electronic Components Volume 2: Diodes, Transistors, Chips, Light, Heat, and Sound Emitters*. Sebastopol, CA: Maker Media Inc., 2014.

Platt, Charles. *Make: Electronics*. Learning By Discovery. Sebastopol, CA: Maker Media Inc., 2010.

Quan, Ronald. *Build Your Own Transistor Radio: A Hobbyist's Guide to High-Performance and Low-Powered Radio Circuits*. New York: McGraw-Hill/ TAB Electronics, 2013.

Reeves, Richard. *A Force of Nature: The Frontier Genius of Ernest Rutherford*. Great Discoveries. New York: W. W. Norton & Company, 2008.

Reid, T. R. *The Chip: How Two Americans Invented the Microchip and Launched a Revolution*. New York: Random House, 2002.

Spilsbury, Louise, and Richard Spilsbury. *Atoms and Molecules*. Building Blocks of Matter. Portsmouth, NH: Heinemann, 2007.

PHOTO CREDITS